BE REAL IN A
THE BEAUTIFUL TRUTH

DARE TO BE DIFFERENT I WANT TO MAKE AN IMPACT WHY FIT IN WHEN YOU WERE BORN TO STAND OUT? NO ONE IS ALL BAD

YOU WERE BORN AN ORIGINAL YOU DON'T SEE THE REAL ME I HIDE BEHIND HEAR ME SEE ROAR ENCOURAGE THE CURIOUS KEEP TRYING BEAUTY COMES IN ALL SHAPES AND SIZES

GOOD VIBES ONLY RULES ARE MEANT TO BE BROKEN CREATE YOUR OWN DESTINY BITE BACK BEAUTY BEGINS THE MOMENT YOU DECIDE TO BE YOURSELF

REBELLIOUS SPIRITS IGNITE REVOLUTIONS THE TRUTH IS COMPLICATED BE THE CHANGE YOU WISH TO SEE IN THE WORLD BE YOURSELF AN ORIGINAL IS ALWAYS WORTH MORE THAN A COPY A LITTLE REBELLION NOW AND THEN IS A GOOD CHANGE THING YOU

BE YOURSELF EVERYONE ELSE IS TAKEN BE ORIGINAL YOU WERE BORN AN ORIGINAL SPEAK OUT I SEE THE BEAUTY IN OTHERS IF IT DOESN'T CHALLENGE YOU IT WON'T

NEVER DOUBT YOURSELF NOBODY IS PERFECT FOLLOW YOUR DREAMS TAKE THE RISK IF YOU CAN DREAM IT YOU CAN DO IT YOU ARE ENOUGH

IT'S OKAY NOT TO BE OKAY BELIEVE IT AND ACHIEVE IT THIS IS ME GIVE ME TRUTH NEVER GIVE UP BE TRUE TO YOURSELF

BE BRAVE DREAM BIG YOUR OPINION MATTERS DREAM CREATE INSPIRE WHAT IS YOUR TRUTH? MAKE US UNDERSTAND THE TRUTH MATTERS EXPRESS YOURSELF

TEEN SPIRIT

Edited By Lynsey Evans

First published in Great Britain in 2025 by:

Young Writers
Remus House
Coltsfoot Drive
Peterborough
PE2 9BF
Telephone: 01733 890066
Website: www.youngwriters.co.uk

Foreword

Since 1991, here at Young Writers we have
celebrated the awesome power of creative writing,
especially in young adults where it can serve as a
vital method of expressing their emotions and views
about the world around them. In every poem we see
the effort and thought that each student published
in this book has put into their work and by
creating this anthology we hope to encourage
them further with the ultimate goal of
sparking a life-long love of writing.

Our latest competition for secondary school
students, The Beautiful Truth, asked young writers
to consider what their truth is, what's important to
them, and how to express that using the power of
words. We wanted to give them a voice, the chance
to express themselves freely and honestly,
something which is so important for these young
adults to feel confident and listened to. They could
give an opinion, highlight an issue, consider a
dilemma, impart advice or simply write about
something they love. There were no restrictions on
style or subject so you will find an anthology
brimming with a variety of poetic styles and topics.
We hope you find it as absorbing as we have.

We encourage young writers to express themselves
and address subjects that matter to them,
which sometimes means writing about sensitive
or contentious topics. If you have been affected
by any issues raised in this book, details
on where to find help can be found at
www.youngwriters.co.uk/info/other/contact-lines

Contents

Islamiyah Girls' High School, Little Harwood

Amira Hussain (13)	70
Ammarah Ilyas (14)	72
Sadiqa Noor	75
Saher Moosa (14)	76
Safa Fathima (14)	78
Yasmina Amin (13)	80
Mariam Yasar (13)	82
Khansa Rehman (13)	83
Ameerah Amin (13)	84
Haya Alkadmani (13)	85

John Hanson Community School, Andover

Emma Pennington (12)	86
Kerenza Hocking (11)	87

La Retraite RC Girls' School, Clapham Park

Abimbola Taiwo (15)	88
Blessing Ofori (12)	91
Kacy Burrowes (13)	92
Oyinkansola Osinlaru (14)	94
Daniella Flores-Escobar (13)	96
Aleena Asad (11)	98
Suray Forbes (15)	100
Nahla-Jai Braithwaite (11)	102
Laverne Akyeampong (12)	104
Sarah-Lee Smikle (12)	106
Nishelle Fernandez (12)	108
Christabel Serebour (13)	110
Onyinyechi Iheme (16)	111
Kendra-Lisa Asare (12)	112
Maida Hussien (12)	113
Emily Edwards (11)	114
Chyianna Miller (14)	115
Abigail Lewis (11)	116
Kaitlyn Rose-Bond-Doyle (12)	117
Angelica Bess-Angol (16)	118
Maryam Raza (11)	119

Elidan Meresie (11)	120
Marie Moore (12)	121
Aminah Haque (11)	122
Asma Hussain (11)	123
Karina Osinlaru (11)	124
Fatima Badjie (12)	125
Nana Eduwa Baffour-Awuah (14)	126
Annamae Tutu (11)	127
Ava Cotton (11)	128
Maya Beale-Springer (12)	129
Luana Leiva (11)	130
Naomi Adeyefa (12)	131
Nanette Afoakwa (11)	132
Aayat Ali (11)	133
Audrey Mensah (13)	134
Maryam Siddiqui (12)	135
Maryam Shoaib (11)	136
Aliyah Campbell-Lee (12)	137
Pison Mulugeta (13)	138
Lara Mahmoud (15)	139
Zahra-Choukri Adam (12)	140
Aarifah Khatun (13)	141
Zoe Almeida Albuquerque (13)	142
Zara-Sophia Simpson (11)	143
Deandra Bennett (11)	144
Zuri Glaze (13)	145
Ashaila Davis (13)	146
Aicha Cisse (12)	147
Audrey Oladejo (13)	148
Savannah Dooknah (12)	149
Khadijah Yaseen (14)	150
Clarabelle Owusu (12)	151
Hafsah Abbasi (13)	152
Amina Doumbia-Cole (12)	153
Melodie Getaneh (12)	154

Merchant Taylors' Girls' School, Crosby

Sophie Sinha (14)	155
Aurora Alba (13)	156
Yan Nok Kristy Wong (12)	157
Isabelle Sprawson (15)	158

Oldbury Wells School, Oldbury Wells

Maddox Dixon (11)	159
Felix Davis (13)	160
Apryl Jennings (13)	162
Darcy Webb (13)	163
James Duncan (12)	164

Park Hall Academy, Castle Bromwich

Aimee Cherry (12)	165
Tyger Willow-Steward	166
Cherri-Marie Hughes (12)	168
Ronita Alo (16)	170
Cordi Savage	172
Lilly-Anna Light (11)	174
Alfie Taylor (16)	176
Libby Rodway (14)	178
Codi Clark (11)	180
Roxi Steward	182
Noah Coleman (11)	183
Danny Naven (12)	184
Rosie Faultless-Hodgson	185
Lacey Palmer (11)	186
Ralph Robinson (11)	187
Maria Avram (13)	188
Phoebe Matthews (12)	189
Chase Wiseman	190
Poppy-May Addison (12)	191
Niamh Watkins (11)	192
Isabel Goodhall (12)	193
Maleehah Millwala (12)	194
Macie Veitch (13)	195
Ruby Anthony (13)	196
Leo Allen-Perks (12)	197
Ariana Wall (11)	198
Nancy Jane McKinley (12)	199
Rose Ellis-Mayes	200
Ava Saunders (12)	201
Bobbie Bluck (12)	202
Humaira Amiri (16)	203

Upton Court Grammar School, Slough

Aadya Sinha (11)	204
Aysha Anfaz (17)	206
Andra-Elena Seghete (16)	208
Rishabh Singhaniya (12)	210
Mahi Gupte (13)	212
Kiaan Maniar (12)	213

THE POEMS

The Balance Of Life

For every good thing that comes, there is the bad,
For all the happiness you get, there is the sad.
For every death that comes, a new person is alive,
For every person who dies in sickness, another will survive.
For every person who unfortunately failed a test,
There will be another who happily got the best.
For every person who tragically left,
There will be another who kindly puts you at ease.
For every person you find fondly caring,
There will be another who is ferociously daring.
For every weakness you don't dare to show,
There's a strength that makes you wildly glow.
For every time you try but you sadly fail,
There will be a time when you triumphantly prevail.
For every time you can't have what you please,
There will be another who would do anything for you, even
travel overseas.
For everything made with the power of creation,
Another thing will be broken by the power of destruction.
For every time you feel life is at its very worst,
There will be another time you want to dive into your future
headfirst.
There's a balance in life, everything is equal,
But unfortunately, for this poem, there is no sequel.

Rebecca Acharya (12)
Grove Academy, Slough

I Am A Bird

I am a budgie.
By day I swoop and sing a charming noise,
But by twilight, I huddle,
Locked in my cage comfortable and happy,
And at night I dream.

I am a flamingo.
By day I drink water with my flock,
Then, I glide around and look for my larva,
Towering above the watery plains,
Searching for a place to nest.

I am an eagle.
By day I hunt my prey,
As swiftly as possible,
Roaming the land where I live,
So my friends follow where I lead,
The Pied Piper of the hunters.

I am a scarlet macaw.
By day I roam alone in the rainforest,
Tweeting as low as I can,
Looking for the best fruits,
I can possibly find,
By night I find the best canopy,
Underneath the stars.

I am an ostrich.
By day I run and spectate the Savannah,
Then I track for plants.
By night I find the best,
Sand and soil to snooze and get some rest.

Taysian Virgo (11)
Grove Academy, Slough

The Seasons

Spring's the first
After winter, forests in thirst
Flowers bloom
Plants return to the room
Spring's always nice
Straight after the leaving of the ice

Summer brings the heat
It's so hot, so take a seat
Finally comes the holiday
"Let's go swimming," we all say
Summer gives us the fun
And also the hot sun

Autumn is next, a gentle sigh
As the leaves let go and fly
Orange hues paint the trees
We start to get cosy as you see
As it starts to get cold
The leaves turn a beautiful gold

Winter, the coldest time
Not playing in the snow is a crime
In the winter's chill, the world turns white
As snowflakes dance in the moonlight
Icicles shimmer like diamonds bright
In this frozen wonder, pure delight

The winter's gone in a ding
And here comes spring.

Dawid Miskiewicz (12)
Grove Academy, Slough

Hopes And Wishes

Hopes and wishes we all have are different,
Different from others like you and they,
Some may have come true,
But the others failed,
Hundreds and thousands of wishes have we,
More than half of them didn't come true,
Our mind bursts with more wishes and hopes,
But we realised later that hopes and wishes are just like guests,
Guest arrive and make us happy,
We spend time together
And then they go away but leave us with lovely memories,
Genies aren't real to grant our desires,
In order to fulfil desires,
All we need is a sincere effort,
Still didn't want to be a coward,
Remembered we still have a long life journey ahead of us,
And it needs to be successful,
Rise up from our fears,
And ready to face them,
As yet we will make our hopes and wishes come true.

Zeest Fatima (13)
Grove Academy, Slough

Through The Storm

In shadows deep where doubts whisper,
A flicker glows, a spark like fire.
The road is long, with twists and turns,
Yet in the heart, a flame inspired.
When storms rumble and skies turn grey,
And dreams feel lost, like ships at bay,
Remember still, the strength you own,
A tale of grit that's yet to unfold.
With every step, though heavy the tread,
Resilience blooms like flowers bred.
For every stumble, every fall,
A chance to rise, to stand up tall.
The mountains loom, their peaks like ice,
Each struggle faced, a step to rise.
So breathe in deep, let courage sing,
For dawn will break, and hope will bring.
Hold fast to hope, let courage steer,
Through darkest nights, your path is clear.
For in the heart that dares to dream,
Lies the power to soar, to beam.

Lorenz Lajara (12)
Grove Academy, Slough

7

The Blinding Truth

Truth.
Is truth the secrets lying inside,
Never shown?
Is truth the pain and suffering time after time?
It's in the past,
Right?
Is truth the positive and negative, the good and bad, the
heroes and villains?
Where do I go?
Is truth the endless tears that run down my face,
Making the light look like endless shadows?
Is truth trying to please everyone,
Family and friends?
Is truth the hopes and dreams that get crushed because of
one person?
Is truth the thought that everything is your fault,
That everything you say leads to disaster,
That even if you put in the work you'll never get there?
Is truth the emotions,
The worry,
The anger,
The love?
But it can also be the hope.

Raquel Pinheiro (11)
Grove Academy, Slough

Friends Leaving Then Getting New Ones

Flowers fly in winter,
Flowers stay in summer,
They always come and go,
Just like people you know,
Some people can leave you,
When you need them,
You give them a second chance but they use you until you leave them,
It might feel horrible but it's for the best,
Just take a rest,

They come for your highest but leave when you're on thin ice,
When you're already used to it,
You feel alone until people come your way and the others come to play,

You finally know that you should have let go,
Then you go into a new school,
And leave those friends and go,
You feel anxious and happy,
You find yourself steady,
You go to new people and they become your besties.

Panna Sumegi (11)
Grove Academy, Slough

9

Green World

Nature is grass,
Nature is big,
Nature is green,
Some people are mean.

Nature is trees,
They are covered in green,
People cut them down,
And they are stuck on the ground.

Flowers everywhere,
Sleeping in their bed,
Lots of different colours,
They travel through the air.

Nature is animals,
Nature is the sea,
Nature is water,
Nature is green.

Splash!
Crush!

Nature is green.

And carrying on,
Look at a frog,
They live in a swamp,
And that's where they belong.

And now we can remember,
What is nature.

One last thing,
Nature is green.

Riley Evans (11)
Grove Academy, Slough

I Don't Like...

I don't like similes,
When I think of them,
My brain melts like cheese in an oven,
My brain is like a vibrating chair,
My heart races like a cheetah.

I don't like metaphors,
When I make some,
My brain is an earthquake zone,
My heart beats at the speed of light,
My stomach is a butterfly cage.

I don't like personification,
When I try it,
Explosions dance in my mind,
Lightning plays with my brain,
Black holes move around in my mind.

I don't like onomatopoeia,
When I use it,
My head goes with a boom and a bam with a pow,
Followed by a kaboom.

Dahunsi Demehin (11)
Grove Academy, Slough

Nobody Else Can Be Me

I am me
Nobody else can be me
Nobody can change me
We are who we are
You are who you are.

You may feel sad, embarrassed
But don't be
Do what you want to do
Be who you want to be.

If you like singing, do singing
Someone tells you to do something
Say no
I am who I am
You, no one or nobody can change it
This is who I am
No one can change that
You can do it
You can be who you want to be

I am me
No one else can be me
Nobody can tell me to be me
Nobody can change me
We are who we are
You are who you are.

Ishpreet Kharay (12)
Grove Academy, Slough

My Family

I have one sister and one brother and, of course, my mum
My sister is 5 years old, my brother is 17 years old
My family means the world to me
Through the hard times, they have helped me
I have been bullied and they were there for me
That's why they mean the world to me
And, of course, my other family
It will take too long to say their names
When I got bullied they supported me
My mum was more supportive, and my dad and stepmum
They are the ones who mean more to me
And my nan and grandad and all my uncles are all
supportive
About what happened
They hated what the bullies were saying to me.

Tia-Louise Hodgeson (13)
Grove Academy, Slough

Nature Is The Beauty Of The World

Nature is beautiful, quiet and serene,
Nature is the forest, with its many shades of green.
Nature is the birds, welcoming in the dawn,
Nature is a calf, struggling to its feet as soon as it is born.
Nature is a salmon, swimming against the stream,
Nature is a volcanic geyser, venting off steam.

Nature is a beast, kicking up a storm,
Nature is the trees, all bent and broken, looking so forlorn.
Nature is lightning striking the ground,
Nature is a forest fire, consuming all around.
Nature is a tornado, with its screaming roar,
Nature is a tidal wave, washing everything ashore.
Nature can be a beauty, and nature can be a beast.

Syed Hussain (12)
Grove Academy, Slough

I Don't Know

I don't know who's real or fake,
I don't know whose advice to take,
I don't know what to do in my life,
I don't know if I should use a fork or knife,
I don't know who I want to be,
I don't know what's wrong with me,
I don't know what I want,
I don't know if I should stay nonchalant,
I don't know if I should speak,
I don't know why I'm so weak,
I don't know why I failed my test,
When I always try my best,
Maybe sometimes it's all in my head,
But I don't know why it continues to spread.

Daria Lewandowska (13)
Grove Academy, Slough

Dreams Of Nature's Animals

I am a dog at night, I sleep in the day
I play, my arms fly up to catch my ball
My owner leaves, I sleep, and when I sleep
I dream that I am a fox roaming in the woods
I hunt for food, hiding from the unknown giants,
My eyes glow at night but at day I dream.

I dream that I am a wolf,
My eyes on my prey, not leaving a single drop
When I attack, my attacks are vicious,
Not leaving things behind
When I sleep, I dream
I dream back home
I wake up seeing my owner come back home,
I run to him to play.

Zoya Khan (11)
Grove Academy, Slough

Pretend

Pretend to be happy,
Even if you don't feel that way.
Pretend to be sad,
And you won't have much to say.
Pretend to be confident,
No one will know how you feel.
Pretend to be mad,
Who knows what you could conceal?

Pretend to be confused or upset,
Pretend to feel remorse and regret.

Pretending to be someone you're not
Being yourself is hard to find.
But if you think about it for one second
What if it's all in your mind?

Pretend.

Naomie Ngwe (13)
Grove Academy, Slough

Cyberbullying

Cyberbullies like to hide
You want to know the reason why?
They hide behind a computer screen
Creating a fake personality
In real life they cannot be mean
So online they show their real me
Cyberbullies can be anyone
Cyberbullies are every size and shape
On a computer screen they are wicked
Inside their minds it's twisted.

Dolshi Rani (14)
Grove Academy, Slough

Why Do We...

Why do we suffer?
Is it because of others?
Why do we need to suffer?
To satisfy others' selfish deeds?
A simple insult can hurt a lot.
Do we hurt because we are hurt?
Like a paper plane.
If we make it wrong, we can't move on.
You are you, you are perfect, nobody is 'normal'.
We are all unique in different ways.
Don't let others shape you.
Why do we try to be different?
You should stay as you.

Jeremiah Gurban (12)
Grove Academy, Slough

Can I, Can You

Can I change myself?
Can you change me?
Can I change the past?
Can you change the past?
I am who I am because of the past.
Do you know me?
I've been through highs and lows,
Struggle and love,
Pain and anguish.
But if it was up to me, we would be
In a forest in a tree.
But I believe I can achieve that,
I can rise up through my lows,
And I will make that happen.
Can I change?
Can you change?

Dominic Hawkins (13)
Grove Academy, Slough

How About?

How about we go on holiday?
Travelling far away...
Not having a care in the world,
Just you, me and the sun.

How about we have a party?
Dancing and singing,
We wouldn't have a care in the world,
Just you, me and the sun.

How about we take a walk together?
Birds of a feather, right?
What if you just ignore me?
You wouldn't have a care in the world.
Just me, myself and I...

Lysette Ngwe (11)
Grove Academy, Slough

Confused?

Should I have breakfast or not?
Shall I have my porridge cold or hot?
I can ponder all day,
These thoughts will forever stay,

Should I order that online?
Shall I make that mine?
My thoughts are all muddled,
I'm totally befuddled,

Should I go to sleep?
Shall I continue to weep?
My thoughts consume my head,
That makes me continuously dread,

Why am I always confused?

Khadra-Jameela Mohamed (14)
Grove Academy, Slough

I Fear

I fear spiders,
I fear heights,
I fear public speaking,
I fear the dark,
I fear everything and everyone,
I *used* to.
Don't say, 'I fear' say, 'I used to fear',
I used to fear spiders,
I used to fear heights,
I used to fear public speaking,
I used to fear the dark,
It's time to face your fears,
I believe you can do it,
So do it.

Lucas Evans (13)
Grove Academy, Slough

Autumn

In the distance, the wind blows,
Rain droplets flood the ground,
Muddy boots stomp and stomp,
Pumpkins scatter round and round,
People come and go,
Branches are laden with berries,
Warm bonfires and sweet cherries,
Vibrant colours and crisp air,
The scent of apple orchards fills the sky,
This is autumn.

Zuzanna Duda (13)
Grove Academy, Slough

I Wonder

I wonder
If the trees can hear me
When I
Scream aloud
Or if
When Dandelion screams
When
I pick him out
There is no telling
Where life can take us
One day
I'm a blade of grass
But today I am myself
Nobody else
Life chooses for me to be me.

Ira Singh (13)
Grove Academy, Slough

On How I'm A Failure

It was one day when I came back home,
And my mum told me I got an F+ in English and my subjects,
I was scared because my dad would ground me,
So, I tried to tell my mum that it wasn't mine,
Then, I wrote a different name,
My parents said, "Oh, okay, you're okay,"
Then, I was okay.

Ahmed Alalawi (13)
Grove Academy, Slough

Affection

Affection is shown when you are born,
Affection can be shown when you are feeling torn.
Affection can be shown when you're ageing,
Turning the pages in life.
But you must put up a fight
For someone in this world worth saving.
Someone does care,
But you might not know they are there.

Ilwad Abdi (12)
Grove Academy, Slough

If You Only Knew

If you only knew,
Knew I was drowning,
Dancing around the ugly truth.
If you only knew...

If you were aware,
Could you bear it?
Have a clue,
Or be so blue?

Seven days, I cried,
Seven days, I pried,
Waiting to get revenge,
But I knew it would be red.

Zainab Ibrahim (11)
Grove Academy, Slough

Stick Man

I am Stick Man
Yep, that's me
I go for a run
And have lots of fun

I sing all day
Laughing along the way
So stick with me
You'll have lots of fun you see

Have some dinner
It's good you see
If you stay with me
You'll have fun you see.

Zaheen Amir (12)
Grove Academy, Slough

How I Feel In My Day-To-Day Life

I love it
Makes my day
All day I appreciate it
Makes my day
It makes my mood
It makes me drool
I get mad when I get bad views
I ain't trying to mess around with you
Like I said before
I ain't trying to tell you what to do but play with my rules
Everything is better
When I get good views.

Muhammad Nawaz (12)
Grove Academy, Slough

What Could It Hide?

Why is it so dark?
Why is it so terrifying?
What could it be hiding?
What will happen if I go inside?
Why should it make me feel like this?
Could I get trapped in there?
Is it safe if I go there?
Will I ever be trapped there?
What could it hide?

Antonia Vasileva (13)
Grove Academy, Slough

Am I?

Am I really happy with life?
Am I really sad sometimes?
Am I really pretty, or is that a lie?
Am I really happy about what people say about me?
Am I really happy with myself?
Am I really that fat?
When will people stop judging?

Michaella Ahlin (12)

Grove Academy, Slough

My Dear Flower

Should I take the flower or not?
Should I keep it or let it rot?
Should I give the flower a home
Or should I leave it to roam?
None of these choices matter to me,
But a pretty flower will always flatter me.

Karla Zincirkiran (14)
Grove Academy, Slough

Future About Yourself

Hi, my name is Fatima.
I always think about my future self.
When I grow up,
I will be a school head teacher.
Protecting students and kids or helping them.
This is my future self.

Fatima Imran (12)
Grove Academy, Slough

Monsters

You don't know what they look like,
You don't know how dangerous they are,
You don't know what they can do if they see you,
You don't know what they do to people.

Yaser Mousa (11)
Grove Academy, Slough

The Bad Day

Maybe you're just having a bad day
Maybe it isn't a bad day
And your day can become good
Just relax, drink water, take a rest
Don't worry, be relaxed.

Julester Fernandes (12)
Grove Academy, Slough

KFC Fried Chicken

Crunchy and fresh,
Tasty and salty,
Served with fries, a perfect delight,
KFC's fried chicken shines bright.
A truly divine meal, pure bliss,
Each bite a savoury, joyous kiss.

Chiarra Gurban (14)

Grove Academy, Slough

My Phone

I watch on my phone
I sleep in my bed
I wake up to watch on my phone
I go to sleep at night
I watch on my phone before going to sleep.

Lena Koziel (11)
Grove Academy, Slough

I Love...

I love feeling joy
I love feeling depression
I love helping people
I love being kind
I love being myself
I love the person I am.

Regis Xhoraj (12)
Grove Academy, Slough

The Broken Heart

The days are gone,
My heart belongs to no one,
I remember those days like it was yesterday,
I remember how my heart fell, never to emerge again,
What if I never see how dumb you could be?
What if all I have is memories?
Then I guess I'm gone,
A broken heart and a broken no one.

Annabelle Botham (12)
Harrytown Catholic High School, Romiley

I Remember

I remember one time I fell,
Back when it was all well,
Putting on a Band-Aid
And watching the scratches fade,
I remember playing in the snow,
Coming home and drinking hot cocoa,
I remember playing with playdough,
Going out to watch streams flow,
I remember asking who liked which boys,
When cardboard boxes were my favourite toys,
I remember being pushed on the swing,
It truly was my favourite thing,
Do you remember your parent tying your shoelace,
Or seeing an old relative and not remembering their face?
I remember playing in the long grass,
Believing time would never pass,
I remember making promises like it was nothing,
Lying to my parents; I was always bluffing,
Do you remember getting in trouble for making slime,
Or being picked up for the last time?
You realise your childhood's passed in a blur,
You don't even remember your dog's fur,
Do not let your schoolwork consume you,
Even though it makes you feel all blue,
Maybe it all went by too quick,
That's the thought that makes me sick,

Don't waste your time
Looking for things to rhyme,
Time truly does fly
When all you're doing is staring at the cloudy sky.

Zuzanna Latańska (16)

Harrytown Catholic High School, Romiley

Expressing Yourself

Expressing - a mask in reverse

I want my thoughts written onto paper,
To show so clearly what I feel,
To myself, am I a traitor?
These thoughts to me feel surreal

How do I offer people these thoughts,
That I, myself cannot sort
Like my ideas will be slaught
Before even asking for support

I want these unruly thoughts to leave,
I desire for someone to know
Though through my mind they will always weave
I guess that's just the way it will go

Nobody understands to be alone
Born to be 'weird', am I in a dream?
Too much time on my own
Like I'm living in my own realm

I want to live - to fly
I feel like a restricted soul
Be it with me or with an ally
Should I have been born with a goal?

My writing I have no one to show
I feel tired in my bones
I feel alone like a crow.

Maja Latańska (13)
Harrytown Catholic High School, Romiley

Red-Streaked Sky

Love is in the air,
My heart is in care,
Knowing the tears are on my face,
Makes me want to end the day.
How could you leave me?
When it was time, it made me want to cry,
Suddenly I look outside and see,
The red-streaked sky.

Annabelle Botham (12)

Harrytown Catholic High School, Romiley

Switching Sides

Why do I keep going?

Listen to my words, they come from your mind.
There's more than mistakes, they're just what you find.
You must now begin to properly try,
And play on every side.

You're thinking too hard, you're just being kind;
Finding someone who cares, there's the bottom line.
Believe what seems best, and all will be fine.
So don't step out of line.

I told you you'd fail, why are you still alive?
The world states such a dunce should just die.
They only claim you're alright to form you as they like.

Why not believe they're right?

Pardon? Excuse me? Are your brain cells alright?

If not, why listen to your part of my mind?

You cannot ignore me, I won't be denied!

Then return another time.
This life is all mine.
Flaws are improvements to find,
No more switching sides.

Jake Thomas (13)
Heolddu Comprehensive School, Bargoed

47

The Glow

There was once a boy as cheerful as could be,
He loved walking in the sand and lying in the sea.
A child without worry,
Who would help in a hurry.
It was now his birthday.
He yelled "Hooray!"
Not knowing the presents he would get that day.

Excited, he opened his gifts,
Until there was only one left, a tiny one that anyone
could lift.
He opened it to reveal,
A present any parent would think to be ideal.
It was a phone.

Day by day, he went on his phone,
Sometimes, leaving his parents to go on his own.
Years went by, and it only got worse,
His parents felt like it was a curse.
They couldn't bear
Their son leaving with only a blank stare.
Their young son was gone.

Consumed by his phone, he didn't know,
That his children had grown up with only a glow.
He wasn't there to help them face
The events like their race.

His children hated him,
He wasn't even there when his son tore a limb.

Now try to remember.
Your family and friends, and don't you dare,
Leave them with a blank stare.

Emily-Grace Rogers (13)
Heolddu Comprehensive School, Bargoed

Don't Lose Yourself To Your Dreams

Sat alone in a painted mess,
Despair filled up my distress.
The mistakes piled high in the room,
Soon enough it would reach the moon.
I glanced around in a panic,
My eyes lingered on a distorted figure,
As they got ready to pull on the trigger.

A gunshot rang through my ears,
And I found myself lost in a mirrored maze.
Reflections of familiar, yet dismembered, figures loomed tall.
As I held on tight and tried not to fall.
I found myself standing in front of a portrait.
It was hung amidst the marble slates.

An eerie smile was painted on,
The girl had determination around her.
Sculpting her dreams out of clay,
My head was filled with corruption,
As I wondered what went wrong.

I found myself in the suffocating room again,
It turned out I was tainted and stained.
I wondered when it began,
Wondered when I lost myself,

And wondered when I was too consumed by my dreams.

Emily Zhu (13)

Heolddu Comprehensive School, Bargoed

Greek Truth

Chaos, the void, the beginning of everything, the start of
the universe,
They created Gaia, the Earth,
Gaia, the Earth, our homes built upon her skin,
Wishing to be reunited with her lover again,
Ouranos, the sky, child and husband of Gaia,
Ouranos, the sky, currently held up by Atlas,
Never to be dropped, for the world would be crushed,
'Your children will overthrow you as you overthrew me',
These words repeated in Kronos' mind as his wife birthed
a child,
These words repeated in his mind as he had overthrown
his father,
Kronos, king of Titans, ate his spawn, for he feared the day
his children revolted,
Despite his efforts, one child avoided this fate,
Zeus, the youngest of the lot, tricked his father into eating
a rock,
His siblings puked out, he took revenge,
He cut his father up with his own two hands,
Banishing his old man into Tartarus.

Lily James (13)
Heolddu Comprehensive School, Bargoed

The World's Greatest Game

Everyone knows about football,
For it is the world's greatest game.
Despite its fun nature,
There are too many things to shame.

Football is no longer a passion,
Football is now about wealth.
Owners think of football as a business
And only ever care for themselves.

Footballers no longer care
And just dive all over the place.
They don't care about the fans' opinions,
Even if they're labelled a disgrace.

Referees are becoming biased
When they are offered money to be.
Players would rather not play
Or just pretend to hurt their knee.

Fans are not innocent either,
Being racist towards players.
Abusing fans and players all the time
And being snappy like alligators.

Racism, death and violence,
It just isn't the same.

Everyone knows what football is,
But is it the world's greatest game?

Kody Price (13)
Heolddu Comprehensive School, Bargoed

Humanity

For hundreds of thousands of years,
Humanity has changed significantly,
And the world is a very different place than it was,
Six million years ago.

Through those hundreds of thousands of years,
There has always been conflict,
And war between different peoples,
And even infighting, from the bloodthirsty Romans
To the expansionist Mongols,
To the unstable Austro-Hungarian Empire,
And so on and so on.

And even now, there is still conflict,
And for all we know, there will always be strife,
For as Albert Einstein said,
"As long as there are sovereign nations
Possessing great power,
War is inevitable."

The way I see it is until we realise we're all on the same rock,
And unite to go forward to the stars,
Then we may stay in the 'loop of conflict'.

Brandon Bryant (13)
Heolddu Comprehensive School, Bargoed

The Minions

The minions,
Cute little dopey guys,
Usually with one or two googly eyes,
What you may not see,
Is the greater power they may be,
Now let them take the lead,
And they'll give you exactly what you need.

Let the minions unite,
So that war can say goodnight.
The minions will play Messiah,
With powers, exponentially higher.

The minions,
Cute little dopey guys,
They're the ones who helped Gru rise,
They probably adore nachos,
As it reminds them of the victory against El Macho,
They're assisted by two 14-footers,
Called Gru and his brother, Dr Nefario,
His name reminds me of an Oreo,
He has a powerful dart gun,
Oh wait, it's a hilarious dart gun.

Now I will see you soon,
Minions, tonight, we steal the moon!

Dewi Miles (13)
Heolddu Comprehensive School, Bargoed

The Teenager And The Teenager

See the cuddling of the teenager,
I think he's angry at the drum major.
He finds it hard to see the ex-boyfriend,
Overshadowed by the reality girlfriend.

Who is that rushing near the school?
I think she'd like to eat the Istanbul.
She is but a calm teenager,
Admired as she sits upon the pager.

Their pleasant car is just a football,
It needs no gas,
It runs on butterball.
She's not alone, she brings books,
A pet dove and lots of schnooks.

The dove likes to chase a dancing,
Especially one that's advancing.
The teenager shudders at the kind petal,
He wants to leave,
But she wants the devil nettle.

Lexie Derraven (13)
Heolddu Comprehensive School, Bargoed

The Truth About Teenagers

They ache, waiting to be heard,
But are too scared to ask for help,
They suffer in silence,
They don't think they are enough,
Slowly breaking.

Someone asks them what's wrong,
"I'm fine," they always say,
Where's their tomorrow?
Living in their friends' shadows,
Tonight, as they look into the sky,
They cry.

Memories are relived,
They tell themselves, "It's okay. Tomorrow's another day."

They grow up,
Life's good,
Reflecting and noticing the change,
A smile appears on their face,
They had a hard time and they lived through it.

Allise Yuile (12)
Heolddu Comprehensive School, Bargoed

57

Who Is Nature?

Nature is us,
We are nature.
We are the draught in the trees,
We are the grass below our feet.
We are the whispers in the wind,
We can be quiet.
We can be loud,
We can be honest.
We can be proud,
We can go with the stream of the river.
Or we can make our own waves,
We can thwart.
We can kill for a thrill,
Or we can stay out of the way.
Or we can jump through the trees with a quiet breeze,
Or we can sail the Seven Seas.
With the seas to our knees,
With a quiet gust of the air.
I am me,
You are you.
We are all of us,
And that's the honest truth.

Aimee Thomas (13)
Heolddu Comprehensive School, Bargoed

The Internet Is Not Real

The internet is not real,
The internet is fake.
Made to make people feel substandard about themselves.
Behind the screen isn't what you see,
Everything is pretend, even me.
All I feel is jealousy,
I know envy is an adverse thing.
And sometimes it feels like a punch on the chin.
Most girls look like their mothers,
The internet makes them want to look like others.
We all have unique faces,
That's what makes us special.
Just because that girl you saw online looked great,
Doesn't mean it's ourselves we have to hate.
The internet is not real,
The internet is fake.

Lola Heath (13)
Heolddu Comprehensive School, Bargoed

I'm Just A Girl

The bows in my hair
And my perfume fills the air
From the frills in my socks
And the way I wear my curls
The mascara on my eyelashes
And the gloss on my lips
The bounce in my walk
And the way I laugh and talk
I'm just a girl
I'm perfect
I'm proper.

The knots of my hair
My perfume makes me sneeze
From the holes in my socks
And the split ends in my curls
The mascara around my eyes
And the cracks in my lips
The limp in my walk
And how I'm too tired to laugh and talk
I'm just a girl
I'm perfect
I'm proper.

Julia Hamod (14)
Heolddu Comprehensive School, Bargoed

The Truth About Social Media

Wearing green that gleams my envy
I let darkness consume me and scroll,
Watching people who are better than me.
This one's in Paris and he's in Rome,
While I'm sat here isolated and alone.
Hours fly by but I don't seem to notice,
I'm like a machine autonomously scrolling,
With the only company being the gleam of my phone.
I realise our relationship is fake and one-sided,
The more love I give, the more hate it throws back.
I'm more than ready to attack,
Humanity kicks in,
Reminding me it's not worth the clicks,
So I let my phone ping, ping, ping...

Rachel Davies (14)
Heolddu Comprehensive School, Bargoed

Beauty Of Nature

Walking through the peaceful woods,
A path to unwind.
Nature's embrace, a solace to find.
Whispers of leaves, a gentle sound,
In the quiet of pine trees, peace is found.

Step by step the mind unburdens,
Amongst the green, the spirit strengthens.
Birds in chorus, a calming song,
In nature's arms, we all belong.

Breathe in the air, pure and light
Nature's therapy, a healing sight.
A repetitive stroll, a mindful art,
Clearing the mind,
A fresh start.

Layla Salter (13)
Heolddu Comprehensive School, Bargoed

Nature's Truths

Through the peaceful woods,
Where the true beauty talks.
The fresh smell of pine trees,
Makes me feel free.
New adventures that are ready to be seen,
Places I've already been.
New paths unfold,
Unleashing me into the unknown.
This peaceful quest,
Is to be guessed.
Leaves blow past,
Leaving a cold blast.
The floral fragrance of wildflowers,
Takes over like sunflowers.
The musky smell of mushrooms,
Leaving flowers to start to bloom.

Kaylyn Woodward (14)

Heolddu Comprehensive School, Bargoed

Nature

From the trees to the bees,
Nature was given to us for free.
Yet we are ungrateful,
Why are we so hateful?
Our world is being destroyed by pollution,
It's time for a revolution!
The air is filled with gases,
Which harm the masses.
There's carbon everywhere,
Do you think that's fair?
We need to crave change,
Or we will be digging our own graves.
We must protect the soil in the ground,
This is our last chance to turn this around.

Kian Christensen (13)
Heolddu Comprehensive School, Bargoed

Dreamers

Dreams are a bewitching thing,
Little stories running through our heads,
We know we can't control them,
But a part of us wishes we can.

Dreams represent messages in our heads,
But it feels like so much more,
They tell you what you really want,
Or sometimes just gibberish.

Dreams are the representatives of our heads,
But should we really listen?

If dreams tell your purpose,
What's your story?

Peyton John (14)
Heolddu Comprehensive School, Bargoed

Dreams

In dreams that seem so hazy,
I picture myself a doctor,
Travelling to all places,
In a uniform, a gown, a smock.

In the city, the mountains, the sea,
As a doctor, I work and work,
Heal them all, cure their disease,
With a stethoscope, a heart full of love.

In a land of fantasy and awe,
With magic and healing powers,
I fix their ills, their pains, their woes,

And spread health to every flower.

Cindy Wu (13)
Heolddu Comprehensive School, Bargoed

The World Of Reading

The world of reading, such a peculiar place,
Every word you read makes a change to the place,
Leave and it will be no fun,
New adventures while you run,
Go and go until the end,
Say goodbye to your new friends,
Then that's the end, but don't worry, you still have time
to spend.

Isabella Wayte (13)
Heolddu Comprehensive School, Bargoed

The Truth Of Nature

There's no lies in nature, only the truth,
The animals are free, just like a tree.
The birds chirp at the roaring river,
Where they will be forever.
The deer hop around and around in the forest where they
are found.
I tie my laces to go new places, but all I see are scary faces.

Tyler Davies (14)
Heolddu Comprehensive School, Bargoed

We Are All Different

Everyone is different,
Everyone is the same,
We are all humans
And life is like a game.
Although we are different,
Heart, skin and brain,
We are all the same.
Everyone is different,
How they look, act and speak,
Everyone is different,
Every face is unique.

Mia Taylor (14)
Heolddu Comprehensive School, Bargoed

Heavy Heart

Has peace always been so loud?
Falling bombs,
The clash of swords,
Empty apartments,
Empty homes,
Never did I think those around me had no value,
So easily discarded,
As though their lives were long overdue,
It's with a heavy heart that I continue,
I hope you understand,
I must mention the sight of widows sighing with heavy breaths,
Holding onto hope that one day it'll end,
Teary faces of orphans
Who have no one left to wipe away the pain,
As young as a month old, fresh out of the womb yet embraced by a level of Maturity no oppressor could ever act against,
The screams of mothers shook the Earth's core, but no sympathy,
If God Himself understood the sorrow and grief then who, as 'peacemaker', Gives us a right to carry on with such chaos, discord and terror?
Only He knows the extremes of the victims' pains,
Me?
No, I'm merely a spectator,
Quietly observing from the sidelines,

Because becoming too emotional is not justice,
Were they really that insignificant?
Shouldn't your heart ache at the sight of such cruelty?
When will the cowardice end?
When will it end?
How many more lives need to be sacrificed before we realise
this is not Peace but an illusion of safety created to keep the
truth hidden,
So I say this once again with a heavy heart,
You're not alone in this fight.

I am with you, God is with you,
We 'should' be with you,
But I'm not promising change,
It is human nature,
Despite a heavy heart, evil has spread like a plague infecting
a once peaceful Utopia of Justice,
We are all corrupt yet no one is truly evil.

And with a heavy heart, I hope we never find a truly evil
oppressor.

Amira Hussain (13)
Islamiyah Girls' High School, Little Harwood

Soliloquy Of A Shattered Soul

Dear specialised reader
To whom this may concern,

When you drown
In the depth of sorrow
What do you see?
A numbness, that itchiness that never goes
A number of angry, anguished souls
A fear that hides and never shows
A fickle never-ending foe

When you speak
With
a
Stutter
a
Stammer
That you refuse
What do you gain?
Only pain
One that you hide, put to shame
Only a false deceitful claim
You made

When you smile
With no teeth
Scared to show around
How do you feel?

An unguarded soldier without a shield
A piece of bloody skin that you peel
A weed amongst flowers in a field
An individual with no item to wield

When you cry
With no light
To guide you
How do you see?
Do you fall with your hands on your knees?
Do you pretend to live life with glee?
Do you fake the 'me' and replace 'we'?
Or do you flee?
And run
To a place
Where no one knows

Why do you place yourself under?
Why do you want to be the light that guides?
But you're stuck as the wax that melts
Why do you want to be the paint that creates?
But you're stuck as the canvas drawn on
Why do you want to be the crack of dawn?
But you're stuck as the birds that constantly move
Why are you different?
Who are you?
What do you do?

The truth is
You are you
As I am me
We are not defined
By who we could be
But instead what we are
And what we do
But you still cry
At pictures
Long lost
To time
And that's fine

But will you believe?

Ammarah Ilyas (14)
Islamiyah Girls' High School, Little Harwood

The Canvas Of My Heart

Emotions are like a river, they flow,
They go high and low,
Every emotion like water, will show,
The beauty in change as we learn to grow.

Joy brightens the night,
While regret extinguishes the light,
Anger erupts like a storm, ferocious and uncontained,
Demolishing a once beautiful landscape and leaving
damage unexplained.

Love breaks the silence, a whisper so loud,
Yet, uncertainty always leaves a doubt,
Hope is like a candle in the dark,
It flickers gently, creating a tiny spark.

Fear wraps around like a heavy shroud,
Sadness covers the sky like a gloomy cloud,
In a world where shadows of sorrow are cast,
I recall memories, still haunted by the past.

Each emotion is a colourful painting with a story to tell,
Inside our heart, they dwell,
Emotions, both resentful and sweet,
Together, they make us complete.

Sadiqa Noor
Islamiyah Girls' High School, Little Harwood

75

Veiled Truths

In bustling lanes where lives collide, the truth is masked in
daily pride,
In morning greetings, mundane chores, in every smile that
opens doors,
In laughter shared behind the walls, where echoes hide in
silent halls,
Truth wears its cloak, both dim and bright, in shadows cast
by day and night.

In schoolyard tales where children play, in office chatter
through the day,
The whispered secrets softly glide, beneath the surface,
truth may hide,
The neighbour's nod, the friend's advice, sincere, yet
wrapped in veiled guise,
Through every glance and spoken word, the lines of truth
are often blurred.

At family feasts where warmth presides, in bustling markets,
life resides,
The truth entwined in every trade, in bonds of trust and
deals they made,
Warm embraces, soothing words, within those folds, the lies
interred,
Truth mingles with the day's delights, elusive in the soft
twilight.

In coffee shops where news is sipped, in headlines where our minds are gripped,
What's true to some, to others bent, the irony in messages sent,
Through daily joys and subtle strife, truth veers and twists within our life, Blurs edges in our mundane sight, yet still we chase its fleeting light.

And so we seek with all our might, through every laugh and silent tear,
The truths we hold may not appear, but still we chase without fear,
For even in the darkest night, the beautiful truth, both shade and light,
Is the veil that blinds our sight.

Saher Moosa (14)

Islamiyah Girls' High School, Little Harwood

The Hope The Fire Kindles

A single spark
A hasty fire
Smokes rising
Embers burning
Velocity increasing
Of elements cracking and crackling

But a few strides away beneath the fog
Stood a melody of a parched throat
Its feathers motionless and exposed
With every spark a chorus composed

The blaze stood in defiance to the resilient note
In a desolate attempt to find the source
As it clothed the living with demise
As anger turned to exasperation

There the songbird
Perched on the rotting leaves
Staring back with empty-eyed resignation
Its voice high as ever, always constant, never-ending
With no sign indicating desperation for flight
Ready to accept the fate ignited

As the fire sears into the flesh
As the feathers wither into dust
The bird utters the last of its trills
As aspiration turns into frills

But in-between the ashes that once fell
Grew a rare wildflower vigour again
As it thrust its way past the barren floor
Waiting for the next fall of a spark
Igniting a wildfire and the flower
To be last to wither again

But this once, the fire recognised its face,
Then amidst the chaos that echoed constant,
In the momentary stillness of its reign,
The fire stopped to listen to the chorus
Sung by the ashes that remained;

And just that once,
Let the notes,
Interrupt,
Its reign.

Safa Fathima (14)
Islamiyah Girls' High School, Little Harwood

Rising From Ruins

In Gaza streets, torn and bare,
Where shadows linger long,
A flower blooms through splitting stone,
Both fragile and yet strong.

The concrete begins to crack beneath,
The weight of years of endless strife,
Yet still, the iris dares to grow,
Clinging fiercely to its life.

Amidst the dust where green once thrived,
Where children once had played,
A single bloom, resilient still,
Prevailed its way to shade.

You cannot silence roots that run,
So deep beneath the ground,
Our voices will rise as petals do,
The beautiful truth will be found.

And though the clouds may veil the light,
And fear may drape our helpless souls,
A spark of hope ignites a flame,
That fuels our cherished dreams and goals.

So, though the road is long and bruised,
And all that's seen is rain,

Golden rays will embrace our home,
And Palestine will rise again.

Yasmina Amin (13)
Islamiyah Girls' High School, Little Harwood

People Of The World

Forced to look their best, never get to rest,
And threatened to be zest.

Even though we live in this toxic environment,
There will always be that one person who is a
disappointment.

Whilst everyone is trying to fit in and be perfect,
I'm struggling over here to see through beauty and defect it.

Depressed and upset about work,
Yet I sit in my chair with a smirk.

Everybody stressed about the future,
While little kids wait to be nurtured.

People putting on a fake smile,
When people from other countries are being exiled.

Through this darkness, some still shine,
With courage and love, our spirits align.

Our lives being put through misery and gloom,
But if we work together we shall bloom.

So to the people of the world I'm writing to you,
Tomorrow I want to see the truth.

Mariam Yasar (13)
Islamiyah Girls' High School, Little Harwood

Two-Faced World

A world that smiles, but frowns inside,
Where shadows hide in broad daylight.
Kind words spoken, but secrets will keep,
Where laughter hides, what makes hearts weep?

A sunny sky, a brewing storm,
Warm embraces that feel cold, worn.
Truth and lies walk hand-in-hand,
With shifting steps on shifting sand.

Promises made, like morning mist,
Fade with the sun, as moments twist.
Eyes that gleam with kindness bright,
But turn away when out of sight.

A friend's sweet face, a stranger's mask,
A simple question, a hidden task.
A painted smile, a whispered doubt,
A welcome in, a shutting out.

Yet still we walk this winding way,
Through every dusk and dawning day.
In this world of light and shade,
Seeking hearts that never fade.

Khansa Rehman (13)
Islamiyah Girls' High School, Little Harwood

83

Fail

She gazed at the corner of her highly strung eye,
Taking shallow breaths, heart skipping a beat.
After which she stared at her hands in fatigue,
Why has she already taken defeat?

She tried to lift up her unused pen,
Her mind swelling with trepidation.
She tried to think but her mind was blank,
Leaving no courage, no energy, no determination.

Time was rapidly running out,
Her weary eyes began to tear.
She tapped her finger to the tick of the clock,
While she clutched her chest in fear.

The bell abruptly rang, the papers were taken in,
It's over, she thought, and deeply sighed.
Her voice was broken, as silent as the grave,
Her mind drowned, closed in, cried.

She couldn't do it.

Ameerah Amin (13)
Islamiyah Girls' High School, Little Harwood

84

My Country, Syria

Precious is your soil, my country.
Your love is the pulse of our blood.
Magic is you and your beauty.
Small hopes blossom in you.

Precious is your soil, my country.
May you live my desired hope.
Free, rising above the buildings.

Precious is your soil, Syria.

May you be free.

Haya Alkadmani (13)
Islamiyah Girls' High School, Little Harwood

Autumn

When I step into the school gate,
The colours of the trees create,
A world of rust-red, orange ochre, pure gold,
A wisp of a curly breeze, a chill starts to unfold,
But my autumn is never going to be shamed,
By all the disadvantages of my autumn being aimed
At from the biting, bitter bullets of the world darting
towards it.
Some may not recognise the true beauty of this gift,
But my autumn is never going to be shamed,
Because my autumn can never be defamed.
The blue, blue skies with butterflies,
Compliment the innocent white clouds like pretty eyes,
The crispy leaves float down, accepting their fall
In the cloudy heavens, all the birds bid farewell,
An arrow pointing south - since the warmth has fallen,
But of course, my autumn can never be shamed,
Since the heat has been tamed.
Many may love it, many may not,
Since many love cold and others love hot,
But listen to me, hear the truth,
Listen to autumn and you'll realise too,
That autumn is beautiful, just like you.

Emma Pennington (12)
John Hanson Community School, Andover

Equality

Why is it that everyone thinks,
Yay, we are all officially equal.
I'll be honest, *we are not!*

If you were a neurosurgeon,
A woman,
And you had a male assistant who handed you things,
Who didn't do anything but look and pass you things,
He would be paid thousands more than you,
Because he is a man.

Women gained the right to vote in 1921,
Women took their lives!
Just so they could write a name on a piece of paper.

When you think 'girl',
You think makeup, dresses, pink,
What if they don't want to be pretty in pink all the time,
What if they want to climb trees and do things 'boys'
normally do?

So, answer me this,
Is this equal?

Kerenza Hocking (11)
John Hanson Community School, Andover

The Burn For Christ

You see,
The burn for Christ we Christians have at the start of our walk,
We put our faith in God the same way Jack put his faith in climbing the beanstalk,
The Bible studies till 1am
What a beauteous relationship we are forming,
The clinginess to the Most High God that holds tighter than a leaf holding onto the branch of a tree in autumn,
We are free, and I can do all things through Christ, who strengthens me.
For the love for God dwells ever so intensely within us
Nevertheless, the Holy Spirit has immensely empowered me to discuss the burn for Christ,
Where has it gone?
Your faithfulness dependent on the stillness of the waves,
But the crazy waves have caused you to have wavy faith,
But that's okay?
Because you have found home in wavy faith, now you're enslaved and can't find an escape,
But the escape
Jesus Christ who is the way, the truth, and the life,
However, you deny him and lead yourself astray.
Children of God, why do you stay so far away from the Lord?
The burn withered away, lifeless, like the leaves in winter dried up, dead,
The fear of it never being revived,

Then we tend to make false truths in our head instead of just entrusting, believing, and putting that 51% of faith into action.
The fire was taken out by the painfully cold night,
The sleepless nights where you question God,
"Why me?"
Nights where you tell yourself it's pointless.
Broken, shattered!
Disconnect, your heart battered down into a pulp,
Why did you stop desiring God?
What's stopping you?
Fear?
The strangling pain that we thought we escaped from?
The deeply rooted doubt that makes us think we should lift high our white flag,
The overly dramatic emotions that stop us from truly believing in the only being that can save us,
Your lifestyle no longer deems evident of the reflection of the Lord but the world only,
You struggle to find the road back,
The path that leads you back to the fire,
You're under spiritual attack,
But did you know that the devil is a liar?
The fire is now dim
Because you never put your trust in him,
You only turn to the Lord when it's convenient for you
And you don't have a clue that...

The Lord is patient
And forgiving
And forever merciful.
But you take advantage of that,
You still dwell in sin
Why bother? Why my sister? Why would you do such a thing?
Aren't you tired of denying the king?
You treat the people around you with evilness, and forget to 'love your neighbour as yourself'
You are lovers of evil, haters of good.
And forget that 'love must be sincere, hate what is evil and cling to what is good'
You say you love God,
But do you love God?
See, God is love
But how can such love be shown when your actions depict those of the enemies?

Abimbola Taiwo (15)
La Retraite RC Girls' School, Clapham Park

The Beautiful Truth Released

Well, everyone thinks they know the truth,
A story fit for pages, established in youth,
Where echoes of laughter danced on streets,
In sun-drenched summers where joy continues.

But there lies in shadows a tale untold,
Of vibrant souls, of hearts bold and gold,
From roots that dug deep in a soil saintly,
Emerges the strength of a long-lost line.

Childhood whispers in shade of deep brown,
In every heartbeat attach into the gown;
Yet beauty blossoms where love has been.

An identity interlaces through trials and arguments,
Of African spirits claiming their life;
Not merely defined by history's chains,
But found in the fires of hope and pain.

So be yourself, let no one erase you,
The rhythm of life that beats with your grace;
For within you lies a soul so bright,
Like the constellations shining through the night.

The truth is not distant; it glimmers right here,
In laughter, in courage, let go of your fear,
Embrace every layer, the dark and the light,
For you are a rocket, what a beautiful sight!

Blessing Ofori (12)
La Retraite RC Girls' School, Clapham Park

91

The Beautiful Truth Of Jamaica

The smell of the curry goat is spicy,
When people smell it, they become hungry and feisty,
Of the wonderful, tasty pure Jamaican culture,
We hear the smooth sound of the steel pan,
You start to move your feet as you open a beer can!

Watching my grandparents playing dominoes is sweet,
In the evening breeze!
As they slam the dominoes on the table,
They look around for Sister Mable,
Holding her notebook and pencil tight,
She checks who's winning, who's losing, who's doing it right!

Having late-night ice cream under the stars,
With the beams of light coming from the cars!
Each lick is a momentum memory of good days,
No bad days, just fun and blessed days.

Jamaica will always be my go-to place to be,
When I need to, but not if I have to!
The colours of black, yellow, and green on our flag tell the
story of strength, creativity, natural beauty, and hope!
We stand tall and strong together, we're no longer tied in
rope,
But thank God, we can now cope!

The white, warm sandy beaches are so inviting,
But be warned that the cold water can be very invigorating!

So come on in, take a dip,
But hold on tight to each other in case you slip!

Picking fresh ripe mangoes from the tree can be a bit
of a battle!
But hold on tight to the branch,
You don't want to end up on the floor of the ranch!

The warm patties with flaky pastry melt in your mouth
While your taste buds are flooded with excitement,
Beef, callaloo, saltfish, and so much more,

You're spoilt for choice, choose any one
Or maybe more that looks good to you,
And bite into the sharp, tasty moistness
As you wait for others in the queue.

Kacy Burrowes (13)
La Retraite RC Girls' School, Clapham Park

The Truth About TV

TV Shows...
TV shows, all sorts of TV shows,
At first, it was Disney and Nickelodeon, before I got Netflix,
I just stuck with what was showing.
Whether it was KC Undercover, Stuck in the Middle, Henry Danger,
Or even those everlasting adverts...

Adverts...
Adverts, all sorts of adverts,
Some were trying to get me to buy washing-up liquid,
Watch a new upcoming movie,
Even buy a new kid's toy with 'parts sold separately',
Which left parents just looking around the room desperately,
At the end of the day, we would be able to agree,
That adverts are *not* a choice, and will *never* be,
But only something which takes up a lot of well-earned time...

Time...
Time, this is an important one,
So much time goes by, which allows my eyes and brain to feast upon the chaos going on, on the screen!
Time I could have spent studying and praying,
Yet I sit there, mesmerised by the content I see in front of me.

Sitting in the corner of my couch binge-eating,
And wondering why every now and then I have to loosen my belt, just a little!

TV...
TV, all the things that TV is:
Fascinating, interesting and almost better than doing anything else.
When you ask me about TV, I will tell you many things, good, bad and ugly,
How it gives my mother headaches,
When she would say, "Turn it off!"

I would look around at the clock and say, "Mother, the time is not enough!"
But I will tell you one thing about TV, it's the truth,
It's the best thing you can do with your time.
The *only* thing I *choose* to do with my time is watch TV.

Oyinkansola Osinlaru (14)
La Retraite RC Girls' School, Clapham Park

A Journey Through Ecuador: Nature's Embrace

In Ecuador's embrace, the coast invites,
Where golden sands and waves unite.
With a gentle hue of gold so grand,
The sand sparkles like stars in a far-off land.
Waves crash while seagulls dance in the sky,
Nature's beauty is a sight to glorify.

The ocean's song, a lullaby so sweet,
In nature's embrace, our hearts find retreat.
Now, in the heart of this ancient land,
Quito stands bold.
Where beauty's tale is millions of years old,
The monument called 'Middle of the World' is at the
world's very core,
Standing proud, a symbol we forever adore.

The mountains stand tall and proud,
Their peaks reaching high, above the clouds.
Their slopes are adorned with vibrant hues,
A paradise for all, with awe-inspiring views.
The air is crisp, the views divine,
A paradise where all wildflowers entwine!
Majestic summits, a sight to behold,
These ancient giants, timeless and bold.

Upon the Galapagos, nature's wonders unfold,
Where unique creatures roam, fearless and bold.
Volcanic landscapes, kissed by the ocean's embrace,
A living laboratory, where life finds its place.
Island jewels, adrift in the Pacific's vast sea,
The Galapagos is a treasure of all time to be.

In the heart of the Amazon, life bursts forth,
Where ancient trees stand tall, reaching for the skies.
Life teems in every layer, from canopy to ground,
In this lush, green world, nature's symphony resounds.
Mighty rivers flow through this wondrous domain,
Ecuador's Amazon, a paradise, forever shall reign.

Daniella Flores-Escobar (13)
La Retraite RC Girls' School, Clapham Park

The Beautiful Truth Of Growing Up

The day I left my mother's womb,
I felt the shine of being welcomed into the world,
The smell of my mother uplifted my spirits,
And a small smile curled.

The day I turned one,
I could make a mess and annoy my mum,
The smell of adventure hit me,
I could crawl, I could clap, I could even slap, leaving my
mum glum.

The day I was three, it was my first day of nursery,
The smell of fun wafted up my nostrils,
But after all the fun I was very thirsty.

The day I was five, I started reception,
Fun-filled was what I thought,
The smell of boredom enclosed the room,
No fun-filled days were sought.

The day I was eight, boredom had sunk in,
The smell of fun and a future came from the bin.

The day I was twelve, I had to wear braces,
The smell of bad breath and fumes left traces.

The day I was fifteen, I went on my first camping trip,
The smell of soil and moss clouded my nose,
While walking made me slip.

The day I was seventeen, I started sixth form,
The smell of sweat clogged my nose,
And I had to share a class with the sweatiest swarm.

The day I was twenty, I finally left those people behind,
The smell of freedom stayed with me;
I had a whole future designed ahead of me.

The day I was twenty-four, I had my own flat,
The smell of independence and hard work drenched me,
This was my new habitat.

The day I was thirty, I had my own child,
The smell of importance and care glowed,
As my little angel smiled.

Aleena Asad (11)
La Retraite RC Girls' School, Clapham Park

The Beautiful Truth Of Being A Twin

The beautiful truth of being a twin,
Is that you always have someone to back you up,
Through thick and thin.

Whether it is the highs or the lows,
Or when other people don't get our jokes,
They are always there and they will keep you close.

Honestly, we wouldn't know who we'd be without each other,
It is a defining part of our lives,

When we walk down the street and see others alone,
We look at them and just sigh.
Sigh, because we know being a twin is amazing!
But whine when the other is being irritating.

I love my twin from the bottom of my heart,
And I would not dare let someone break us apart,
She was the upstart of my life,
Takes care of me even when no one is in sight,
Guarded me from terrible nightmares,
When I was frightened in the thick darkness of night.

I'm not going to lie; I can't praise my sister throughout this whole poem,
Because I need to highlight that she can be so annoying.
She always thinks that she is right, going on and on,
I cannot stand it, when sometimes she treats me like a newborn.

Nagging just like my mom, it never stops!
Her sharp tongue slices through my argument,
Whenever she thinks I'm wrong,
Regardless of the time of day,
She finds a way to shut me up either way.

But let us leave this poem on a good note,
Because I want to promote,
That she helps and encourages me,
With so much growth.

Suray Forbes (15)
La Retraite RC Girls' School, Clapham Park

My Outstanding Mother

My mother is full of mixtures,
She's almost like an idea from a science lab!

She can never stop pouring her mixtures of love, caring
And using her Nigerian trait, with the notion,
She'll never be late!

We pray in the morning, we pray in the evening,
We pray over our food, oooh that's some seasoning!

I love her cooking, the taste is so sweet, just like her heart,
I love her food, that tastes so warm, just like her,
Like a warm hug from a mug!

I ask God to show me the gift that He has given me,
Then my mother appears, right in front of me!

She is my gift, as I am her gift from our father,
Day and night I can always sleep tight,
Knowing there is a roof over my head,
Day and night I know by God's grace,
That there's always enough!

Just like how I support my neck,
My mother is the head of my house,
Her bold, strong love will never alter,
But will always give me shelter!

A mother's love is the ultimate sacrifice,
For she gives everything she has for her children!

Dear Holy Father, thank you for my mother,
For those who don't have one,
I pray a mother figure comes into their life,
Amen!

Nahla-Jai Braithwaite (11)

La Retraite RC Girls' School, Clapham Park

The Beautiful Truth About Life

Has anyone ever told you about the beautiful truth
about life?
I believe not!
Some people focus on the downfalls of life,
So, most people don't know or think about,
The beautiful truth about life!
Let me tell you about the beautiful truth about life,
There is no such thing as I can't,
If you think you can't, you won't be able to do it,
What you want to do in life!
Even if people doubt the things you can do,
Don't let that wash away your dreams,
Because that will make you feel more worthless!
Disability is not inability, once you have a talent, you have
a gift!
Some people will try to discourage you from your dreams,
Because they think it's worthless, but remember,
Every gift is unique!
It's alright to cry or feel hurt,
God never promised a day without sorrow or pain,
He promised us light through life and comfort for our tears!
Give your heart to those who need a little push now and
then,
Kindness, patience, and confidence are worth more than
anything in the world!

So, every time you realise someone needs comfort,
Just give them a little smile to show you care.

Laverne Akyeampong (12)
La Retraite RC Girls' School, Clapham Park

The Beautiful Truth Of Distance

We all act like we don't care,
We all act like it's not there,
We don't want to be left in despair,
Because distance is everywhere.

Distance! They were once your best friend through thick and thin,
Now you don't even exchange a grin,
They disappeared not a letter, not a text,
Not knowing what's going to happen next!

Once a friend, now a stranger,
You've never met, first hello,
Now goodbye,
Should I give it one last try?

Distance! Once they were here, now they're gone,
Your father, your mother, your brother, your son,
Time keeps passing by, memoirs stored up,
Now released from your mind,
Trying not to forget before you run out of time!

Distance! You don't know what it's like,
For every day to go back in time,
Every hour of the day,
All the memoirs on replay.

We all have that one room,
Once we set our gaze all the memoirs come rushing back,

One by one, two by two,
You can never forget what you've been through!

Everything happens for a reason,
If you look deep enough, you will see one!

Sarah-Lee Smikle (12)

La Retraite RC Girls' School, Clapham Park

My Beautiful Journey

From Sri Lanka to England, London,
What a journey both me and my family have encountered,

With brave hearts, and bold determination,
We felt empowered to go forward, always forward!

Days and months passed quickly like the wind,
By now our new minds became combined!

As we ventured dark and deep into the unexpected
obstacles of life,
We looked around, everyone is kind!

As we stood holding each other's hands together, we felt
fearless, powerful, even invincible!
We could do anything together!

When I started my secondary school, I felt almost like a fool!
I was scared and nervous, but had purpose!

As I looked back on my life, I thought to myself that I had
come so far
and to give up now would be meaningless!

I took a deep breath and stepped inside, I had so much
pride!
I met my classmates, who didn't have to translate,
I met my teacher who showed me the procedures,
I felt so happy, everything was so snappy!
Soon enough I made some friends,

Now is the time I can stand back and comprehend the appreciation of imagination, and education!

Nishelle Fernandez (12)

La Retraite RC Girls' School, Clapham Park

The Beautiful Truth Of Ghana

In West Africa's heart, where the sun shines bright,
Lies Ghana, a treasure, filled with pure light,
From colourful markets to the beat of the drums,
The spirit of joy in every song hums.

The smell of jollof fills the warm air,
Fufu and light soup - a tasty affair,
Kente cloth flowing, bright and bold,
Each pattern tells stories of tradition and gold.

Lively music plays, highlife and hip-life,
Inviting us all to dance, joy in our lives,
The flag stands tall, red, yellow, and green,
With black in the centre, a proud sight to be seen.

Red for the blood of those who fought for the land,
Yellow for the wealth and the future we planned,
Green for the forests, rich and alive,
Black for the people, strong and to thrive.

With beauty around us, from land to the sea,
Ghana welcomes all with warmth and glee,
As the sun sets in Accra, laughter fills the night,
In this lovely land, our spirits take flight,
Here, love unites us, in joy's endless light.

Christabel Serebour (13)
La Retraite RC Girls' School, Clapham Park

In Her Eyes

In her eyes lies the doubt behind her beauty,
The constant wondering if she would ever be good enough.

In her eyes lies the uncertainty of her beauty,
The constant pulling at the chains of society that wanted to bring her down.

In her eyes lies the pain behind her beauty,
The constant voices in her head telling her she will never be what she strives to achieve!

In her eyes lies the pain behind her beauty,
An aching heart with endless tears.
But that was what used to be in her eyes!

Now, in her eyes lies resilience,
The constant reminder that she is good enough.

In her eyes lies *power*,
Breaking every chain that tried to pull her down!

In her eyes lies *determination*,
Wiping her tears and uprooting the self-hate that was planted in her heart!

Those are the eyes of a beautiful young girl who struggled to find herself,
Now she is found, nothing can stop her!
Because in her eyes lies the truth behind her *beauty!*

Onyinyechi Iheme (16)
La Retraite RC Girls' School, Clapham Park

111

The Mystery Of Me

In the garden of my mind, where petals softly sway,
Exploring depths of a distant bloom, a journey day by day.
Unveiling hidden layers, roots embracing the unknown,
The truth in every flower, beautifully shown.

They don't know my name!
I'm a blossom, a picture without frame.
They don't see my sunshine, nor my rain,
To them, I'm just another petal, caught in the grain.

My soul, a vibrant canvas,
Reflecting on the past, embracing every time,
Through colours and scents, my essence takes flight,
In the mystery of me, blooming in plain sight.

I am a flower in bloom,
My petals are closed off to the unknown,
Protecting my heart from days of gloom,
For they hold stories that may never be shown.

When my flower begins to open,
It leaves some of my words unspoken.
My colours whisper secrets untold,
In this Tradescantia pallida, a mystery to behold.

Like shadows dancing in the moon's soft glow, it blooms.

Kendra-Lisa Asare (12)
La Retraite RC Girls' School, Clapham Park

Quiet Down...

I struggle to do my job as a teacher,
it is always like I am in violent waters in a paper!

It feels like I cannot go a day
without saying the same words,
"Quiet down!"

Sometimes I just wish that everything would go silent,
and I would feel serenity,
yet I always struggle to just get them all to,
"Quiet down!"

Forever everlasting screams and chatting of the students,
sometimes I just wish that they would all just,
"Quiet down!"

Now I get it to all those teachers as a child,
I get why now you just need them all to,
"Quiet down!"

All those years ago, now I get it,
sometimes the world just needs to be quiet,
to reach silence, to reach happiness,
to reach the dream world,
Silence.

That is why we all just need to,
Quiet down...

Maida Hussien (12)
La Retraite RC Girls' School, Clapham Park

113

Jamaica

Jamaica, sweet Jamaica!
Listen to the sound of the waves
The beautiful sun shining on my face
I look over and see the palm trees swaying
As the breeze gently whispers, "Are you staying?"

I play out with my younger cousins, I can smell my
grandma's cooking
We all look around and wonder why everyone is looking
But the aroma of the cooking, and the mixing of the breeze
Brings a cool vibration, what a great sensation!

I love old sweet Jamaica, there's no place I'd rather be!
With sweet reggae music, and the warm sea breeze
This paradise island, full of everything you'll ever need
You can close your eyes and drift away on a journey only
you can see!

As the night draws in, and the fireflies start to sing
They light the path with nature's light, as the glow reaches
as far as the eye can see!

The distant humming, the local sounds,
Big up Jamaica! Be happy you were found!

Emily Edwards (11)
La Retraite RC Girls' School, Clapham Park

Heart To Heart

The truth is beautiful when everyone stands heart to heart,
In a world of echoes I stand apart,
A canvas of colours, a unique world of art,
While others march in a uniform line,
I dance to the rhythm of my own design,
The truth is all I will ever hold,
Not bound by the norms that others uphold,
So here is for the unique, the spiritual, the free,
For being ourselves is the key to be,
I carve out my journey, I set my own pace,
While others may follow the paths that they trace,
In shadows where secrets often hide,
The truth emerges, a relentless tide,
It cuts through the silence as sharp as a knife,
Revealing the truth of everyone's complex life,
With truths like wildflowers, they bloom in the sun,
Embracing the shadows, I know I am one,
In the dance of existence, let honesty reign,
For the truth when uncovered brings freedom from pain,
The truth is beautiful when everyone stands heart to heart.

Chyianna Miller (14)
La Retraite RC Girls' School, Clapham Park

The Truth Of My Jamaican Heritage

The day I opened my eyes, the day Jamaica was revealed to
me, I looked and sighed,
Life and beauty filled my heart, I knew this was a great
start!
The day I turned ten, I knew my life here would be off the
charts,
This is my life, my world, and everything I see,
All this in me is pure glee!
My religion is the place I should be,
With the Lord on my side, you can't touch me!
This is my place, my world, my peace,
This is the place I am meant to be,
The language sings like a bird singing in the trees to me,
With all the tones and cones, it's like ice cream to me!
The sounds and smells swirl around like a bell, but who can
tell, it's inside my cells!
The beautiful smiles of every person circled like a ring,
The sun of Jamaica made all the birds sing.
The sun doesn't always shine,
but the tears of people will always be mine!
This is my heritage, we are the Jamaicans!

Abigail Lewis (11)
La Retraite RC Girls' School, Clapham Park

A Scary Truth

A scary truth is hard to face,
It lurks in the shadows, without grace,
We try to hide, just take a look at my face,
We try to run but it catches up to us, we look around, there's nothing more to discuss!
If truths were lies, and lies were truths, we wouldn't want to listen or use our Bluetooth!
The bitter truth can be scary, but as you listen, it seems eerie!
It gives us all a chill, but doesn't kill,
It just gives you a heads-up, you soon become aware, so you feel you should share,
All these emotions are key in life, you stop and think hard before you pick up the knife!
Is there something around that corner, or are you simply a moaner?
Try not to be silly, your name is not Billy! Try to be brave, you're not trapped in a cave,
Embrace the scary truth with a smile, showing your teeth, stop looking underneath!
Remember the truth will set you free, so go for a walk, and hug a tree!

Kaitlyn Rose-Bond-Doyle (12)
La Retraite RC Girls' School, Clapham Park

Ambition And Success

Ambition and success come with a lot of stress,
Trying to impress everyone around you so you don't look a mess,
Trip-ups and falls will happen,
It's a part of life's test,
Making sure your career path is for you, so you won't regret,
If you keep your head down and keep things all about you, do you think you'll lose your friends?
Cut some ends, lose some friends, and hopefully one day you'll make amends,
Being selfish about your success is what you need,
Sitting around the table while life is throwing tricks at you like a game of chess,
You can dream to be a doctor,
You can dream to be a vet,
But only you can change that,
So don't follow the rest,
Invite the fearless foot to scale,
The stairway towards the sky,
Rise, rise, rise, rise,
Never look back!
Never lie!
Work hard and never give up,
Time will blow by!

Angelica Bess-Angol (16)
La Retraite RC Girls' School, Clapham Park

The Beautiful Truth About Me, Myself And I

I might be cruel, but I might be kind
I might be silly but trust me, I can use my mind!
I might be sad, but I might be happy
I always walk into school gladly
I might be weak, but I might be strong
If you'd known me, you'd know that I am not always wrong
I might be impossible, but I might be adaptable
But for my age, I know that I am very sensible
I might be bossy, but I might be a listener
However, no one can be the perfect daughter
I might know it all, but I might be confused
But please don't call me dumb, that's just wrong
I might want to be a businesswoman,
But I also want to feed the homeless,
I know whatever I do, I will be successful
I might be confident, but I might be scared
Everyone should know, one way or another, you can do it
If you just believe in yourself and have little fear.

Maryam Raza (11)
La Retraite RC Girls' School, Clapham Park

Ashenda Festival Poem

A shenda, a blaring cultural girl's event in the
S ummer.
H efty hair swayed like the trees in the wind,
E veryone danced in unison whilst the music played,
N atty dresses shone in the bright hazy sunset,
D azzling henna patterns gleaming like a church window.
A cascade of colours twirled into the moonlight.

A shenda, cultural food and amazing flavours
S mell the sensation, hear the sounds and more!
H olding hands as we listen to the drums, swaying side by
side as we stand,
E choes of laughter rushing through the air, stop and
think, for a minute if you dare!
N ever-ending food and drinks for three days,
D ashing, when you look closely it's quite catching,
A udience going house to house, slowly moving like a
mouse.

Elidan Meresie (11)
La Retraite RC Girls' School, Clapham Park

My Beautiful Truth

In a tapestry woven of stories untold,
Black hair dances in shades of bold.
Coils and kinks, a symphony of grace,
A crown of resilience, a proud embrace.
From silken waves to vibrant afros,
Each strand whispers secrets that only it knows.
With every twist and turn, history unfurls,
A canvas of culture, a treasure of pearls.
Sunlight catches on braids, glistening bright,
Each plait a journey, a celebration of light.
In textures diverse, beauty is found,
A harmony echoed in the soul's profound sound.
Through trials and triumphs, it stands with pride,
A testament to strength, a heart open wide.
From barbershop chatter to salons aglow,
The power of black hair, a force that will grow.
So let us honour this crown we all wear,
In every hue, in every layer,
For black hair is more than a style to adorn,
It's a legacy cherished, a heart reborn.

Marie Moore (12)
La Retraite RC Girls' School, Clapham Park

121

Flowers

Flowers are beautiful and pretty,
They smell sweet and sometimes fuzzy!
They come in all sorts of colours, shapes, and sizes,
Blue, green, others, and even white, like mice!

They glow steadily and beautiful in your garden,
At different heights, they catch the light!
Each raindrop packed with pure delight,
With nutrients and moisture, to strengthen those stems,
We wait and watch as nature condemns!

Make sure you look after them, or else they will die,
They might start to rot if not in the right pot!
Or might even attract flies, especially when you're out
of sight!

For every flower you have seen,
A seed was sown to attract the bees,
So have a look so you can see,
The beauty and majesty of colours, shapes, and smells,
that we all see!

Aminah Haque (11)
La Retraite RC Girls' School, Clapham Park

The Land Of Olive Trees

In the shadows of sacred soil, blood does stain,
Voices of children lost, a mother's pain,
Little hands grasp at dreams, torn apart,
Genocide's cruel grip grounds every broken heart,

Olive trees weep, their branches bent low,
Families long for comfort, where hope struggles to grow,
All at once vibrant, now cloaked in despair,
Innocence shattered, humanity grasping for air,

A baby's last breath gasping for air
How is this okay? How is this fair?
Screams of agony ring out every night,
Living in this cruel world is a terrible fright!

But through the pain there is a streak so bright,
That freedom can bring back this land's light,
Gone would be all the hardship and sorrow
And at last we can wake up to free land tomorrow.

Asma Hussain (11)
La Retraite RC Girls' School, Clapham Park

My Beautiful Mother

My beautiful mother, tall and proud,
Who always stands out in a crowd!

I would never dare to see her different,
She's like a magician going from best to best,
But always loses because sweetness can't rest!

I always ask God for something good,
He gives me something each day so true! My mother.

People say angels are only in Heaven,
But it makes sense, when my mother was made seems like
an angel fell instead!

If I were damned of body and soul,
I know whose prayers would make me whole!

In her eyes he placed bright shining stars,
In her cheeks fair roses, you see;

God made a wonderful woman,
And gave that dear woman to me!

Thank you Mother for being my rock,
My confidence and my best friend.

Karina Osinlaru (11)
La Retraite RC Girls' School, Clapham Park

124

Echoes Of Reality

In the dawn's embrace where shadows flee a whisper of truth dances wild and free,

The sun spills gold on the waking Earth, revealing the beauty of life's quiet worth,

Each leaf a story, each breeze a sigh, nature's soft secrets beneath the vast sky,

In laughter and tears, in a moment we share, the truth finds a voice, a melody rare,

Through trials we wander, through joy and through pain, in the heart our struggles, our truths we regain,

With every heartbeat, with every glance, we uncover the beauty in life's fleeting dance.

So, we cherish the moments, both bitter and sweet, for the truth is a treasure, a gift we repeat,

In the tapestry woven of love and light, the beautiful truth shines ever so bright.

Fatima Badjie (12)
La Retraite RC Girls' School, Clapham Park

A Lie, A Whole Lie, And Nothing But A Lie

I thought it was just a figment of imagination,
The corruption,
The desire to rule all the nations,
People acting on how they feel,
Being fake and never real,

They cultivate a habit of lying,
They don't care for the millions who are dying,
The mothers and children who are crying,
They are like predators on their prey, always prying,

But what would happen if you took a stance,
Call them out in a single song or dance,
Break them free from the chains of slavery,
Speak on wrongdoings loud and hastily,

Billions of lives depend on you,
But what will you decide to do,
Billions of voices are yet to be heard,
Are they silent
Or were they silenced?

Nana Eduwa Baffour-Awuah (14)
La Retraite RC Girls' School, Clapham Park

My Mum

My mum, we bond, she's strong!
She never leaves my side, never lies,
She's my number one mum!

Her hair moves like the sea,
Her eyes shine like a star,
Her shoes shine and twinkle side by side!
She walks like a queen with a crown on her head,
She's a superstar, who drives a car!

She helps me because she loves me with all her heart!
I always look up to my mum, she reminds me of a lark,
Like a beautiful butterfly, letting her feelings out!

Like mother, like daughter, we're like peas in a pod,
Like the moon and stars, like the sky and sea, like Adam
and Eve!

Who needs a best friend, when you live with the best.

Annamae Tutu (11)
La Retraite RC Girls' School, Clapham Park

My Amazing Parents

I love my dad; he makes my days brighter!
Even when I'm happy, he makes me smile a bit wider,
I love my mum as much as I do he!
There is no one quite as loving as she,
I love my sister, though she's a bit crazy,
She's even less tolerable when she's lazy!

I love my older sis - she's funny and free,
She doesn't care what other people think of me!
I love my older brother, who's in university today,
When he graduates I'll shout, "Hooray!"

I love Natasha, who's very sweet,
I even remember the day we did meet,
Finally, my little brother, though not yet born,
We will never be separated or torn apart.

Ava Cotton (11)
La Retraite RC Girls' School, Clapham Park

The Beautiful Truth Of Love

Love is such a complex emotion,
It cannot be discarded or changed like a potion.
It is the purest of pure,
A thing you want of more,
And it will never, ever be a bore.
It can also be hard,
A thing you should guard,
Just like that precious Valentine's Day card.
It is free to love,
Free like a dove,
Soaring over the cities above,
But sometimes people neglect,
And sometimes forget
That love cannot be bought,
Nor can it be caught!
For it is a tricksy thing,
Like that summer fling.
So hold on to love,
Don't give it a shove,
Or let it slip through your fingers,
Hold on to it through those cold, dark winters.

Maya Beale-Springer (12)
La Retraite RC Girls' School, Clapham Park

129

My Amazing Parents

I love my dad; he makes my days brighter,
Even when I'm happy, he makes me smile a bit wider,
I love my mum, as much as I do he,
There is no one quite as loving as she,
I love my sister, though a bit crazy,
She is even less tolerable when she is lazy.

I love my older sis, she is funny and free,
She doesn't care what other people think of me,
I love my older brother, who is in university today,
When he graduates, I'll shout "Hooray."

I love Natasha, who is very sweet,
I even remember the day we did meet.

Finally, my little brother, though not yet born,
We will never be separated, or even apart, torn.

Luana Leiva (11)
La Retraite RC Girls' School, Clapham Park

My Beautiful Mother

The beautiful truth of my mother is never unknown,
She helps me with my difficulties, especially when I feel
alone,
She's beautiful inside and kind down to her feet,

I love her with everything in me, and I know that she equally
loves me!
We talk together and laugh together; we even laugh
hysterically!
To have a friend so beautiful and bold, it's almost like a
story never to be told!

My mother, my mummy to the end!
We pray, praise, and worship the Lord together,
We attend our church every week and will do so forever,
We learn our hymns in the name of the Father, the Son and
the Holy Spirit! and will continue forever and ever, *Amen!*

Naomi Adeyefa (12)
La Retraite RC Girls' School, Clapham Park

The Beautiful Truth Of My Mother

My mother has always been as beautiful as the dark blue sky!
She has always been there for me, especially to make me try!
No matter how many times we'd have an argument,
We would always find extremely deep sentiments,

As I grew up, I started to realise that a mother's love is as strong as metal,
Just like to make tea, we all need a kettle!
No matter what was done or said that day,
We would always find the time and space to respect another day!

Now that she is getting older, she can no longer bring me on her shoulders,
But we sing, laugh and dance all day, and we give thanks and praise to The Most High who without Him, we couldn't fly!

Nanette Afoakwa (11)
La Retraite RC Girls' School, Clapham Park

Books!

Books, books
Fill the page as an image fills on the stage
Heroes and villains have so much emotion
Which always causes so much commotion!

Laughing, crying, cheerful fun,
But the book is always done, done, done
So, it's time to move on to the next one
Open, close, flip the page
Words fill out on stage!

Drawing illustrations, smiles and frowns,
Tears on the page will always make you cry out loud
The cover's always so bright like the sun
But on the inside...

Words, words, words
Vocabulary expands,
Every page you scan,
Your mind relates as it imitates
The words and sounds you accumulate!

Aayat Ali (11)
La Retraite RC Girls' School, Clapham Park

My Beautiful Truth

What possibly could be my beautiful truth? It's my melanin!
Glowing mahogany in the sunlight, and beautiful hazel in my eyes!
Nothing can waver my confidence with my amazing melanin!
It's *my* melanin!
The brown that once had to be set free, so why can't I show my freedom?
What even is my freedom? It's my melanin!
How can my melanin be my beautiful truth? It's the truth!
The truth about all the enslaved people who were confined to unpleasant environments
Because of their chocolate-covered skin!
It's my Beautiful Truth,
The truth about our venture around the earth to find truth!
Melanin, my beautiful truth.

Audrey Mensah (13)
La Retraite RC Girls' School, Clapham Park

My Beautiful Family

In a cosy home where laughter rings,
Lives a family bound by love's sweet strings.
With Grandma's wisdom, a guiding light,
Her stories weave through day and night.

Four siblings play, with joy they share,
In games and dreams, they show they care.
Each unique, yet together they stand,
A vibrant crew, a united band.

Mum's gentle touch and Dad's strong embrace,
Create a haven, a warm, safe space.
Through ups and downs, they face the tide,
In this family circle, love won't hide.

Eight hearts entwined, a tapestry bright,
In every moment, they find delight.
Through laughter and tears, they journey on,
In the heart of their home, love's never gone.

Maryam Siddiqui (12)
La Retraite RC Girls' School, Clapham Park

Mask

Make me a mask so I can be,
The person who I want to be,
Make it pretty and make it bright,
To keep the real me, out of sight

Make me look better than before,
Make me the same, but so much more,
Change my appearance, change my name,
Give me the courage to play the game

Paint me with indigo, paint me red,
Every colour in my head,
Snark, dramatic, angry, bright
Every emotion hiding in plain sight

But hide-and-seek is a lonely game,
Perhaps I'll wait until you call my name,
Perhaps I'll trust that you don't see,
The mask on my face, you just see me.

Maryam Shoaib (11)
La Retraite RC Girls' School, Clapham Park

My Mum

The most beautiful mum in the world, to me,
Inspiring, caring, loving and kind,
My mum is always there for me when I'm happy or sad, and
she always makes me feel better,
I feel so blessed to have a wonderful mum, and I thank the
Lord every day.

My mum is the first person I see in the morning, which
makes me happy,
I thank my mum for always praying for me,
If I could choose a mum, I would choose you all over again,
You're the sunshine to light my day.

Her tender smile guides my way,
She means the world to me,
All the time she will be there for me,
I love you, Mum!

Aliyah Campbell-Lee (12)
La Retraite RC Girls' School, Clapham Park

The Beautiful Truth Of My Family

My beautiful truth is my family.
From my precious mum to my caring siblings,
If I had a chance, I wouldn't change a thing.
My mother always believed in me when I was brought down,
She would always hug me and say it's alright,
My mum made sure I was loved and would always be my best friend.
My dad always made sure I had a roof over my head and had what I needed,
Every sweat my dad shed was gold in my eyes.
I saw his exhaustion and love for us.
My brothers are annoying sometimes, but they love me,
They would save up their money to spend on all of us.
This is the beautiful truth for me.

Pison Mulugeta (13)
La Retraite RC Girls' School, Clapham Park

The Beautiful Truth Of The Land Of Peace

In the land of peace
Where a war will never cease

I pray for you!

I know the prayers are overdue
I hope I find a land as beautiful as you
Perhaps it's a clue
Of how I feel blue

In the land of peace
Peace is dead.

At least your beauty was said
Before there was bloodshed

In the land of peace,
Peace is dead.

The land has bled
I can only dread
The day that the land is all red

The Land of the Olive
I will never forgive
I am only sad that I will outlive the beauty
Of the land of peace.

Lara Mahmoud (15)
La Retraite RC Girls' School, Clapham Park

139

A Mother's Love

I have seen a rainbow circle around the sky,
And I have stood on a mountain,
And watched an eagle fly,
I have seen trees in a meadow,
Shelter the morning dove,
But I haven't seen anything,
To match the wonder of a mother's love,
I have seen a sunset,
More beautiful than gold,
I have stood on a rose bed,
And watched leaves unfold,
I have seen so many wonders,
And blessings from above,
But I haven't seen anything,
To match the wonder of a mother's love,
No, I still haven't seen anything to match the wonder of a
mother's love.

Zahra-Choukri Adam (12)

La Retraite RC Girls' School, Clapham Park

Imagine A Place

Envision a place,
A place which knows all,
A place which remembers all.

Visualise a place,
So vast and free,
Full of fascinating things to learn and see.

Picture a place,
A place which holds trouble,
A place with everything imaginable.

Fantasise a place,
A place which has aged and is mature.
A place with all ages from the elderly to the immature

Well, there is a place,
A place which holds many memories,
Worries and journeys.
It has many regrets, but it never forgets,

And that place is called the Internet...

Aarifah Khatun (13)
La Retraite RC Girls' School, Clapham Park

The People's Apple

Just like the brain,
An apple is determined,
Just like the heart,
An apple is delicate.

It can be sweet,
It can be sour,
Its aroma is so inviting,
You can't resist biting into it!

The crunchy bite of the apple,
And intense juicy, tasty flavour,
Will keep you coming back for more,
Like a roller coaster.

Its intense red colour,
Can be appealing to the eye,
But rotten on the inside!

But if you find the right apple,
It can be the sweetest thing you meet.

Zoe Almeida Albuquerque (13)
La Retraite RC Girls' School, Clapham Park

The Truth

What is the truth?
How beautiful Earth is?
How wonderful life is?
How easy learning is?
Well, the truth is,
This isn't the truth.
These things aren't as wonderful or perfect as you think
The real truth is that
Learning is never easy,
It is a learning curve.
The Earth is not that beautiful,
We are destroying it by the second.
So is life that wonderful?
In conclusion,
This is not the truth,
The truth is what we make it.

Our truth!

Zara-Sophia Simpson (11)
La Retraite RC Girls' School, Clapham Park

My Truth Of The Day Of Remembrance

In the lonely fields stands a vibrant red flower,
In remembrance of the soldiers who died for us and others who expired,
They opened our hearts so we can live forever,
Oh, how I love that red flower, that beautiful poppy!
You live in our hearts forever!
Where you grew on that field, it was like a little army coming to life!
And now every year, everyone can draw near and remember the brave who cared!
And when your true colours were shown, it was like those colours were blinding me by the sight!

Deandra Bennett (11)
La Retraite RC Girls' School, Clapham Park

My Home

A place that I call home,
Where the water is always clear
I'm never scared to roam
It's where I know I belong
Every street I walk just feels so strong,

I walk down the road, and I start to smile,
It's my home where I feel worthwhile
Laughter fills the air and happiness grows,

It's where everyone's joy really shows,
Home is where I feel safe and warm,
It's my world, it feels just right,
It's a place to hold me close and tight

Zuri Glaze (13)
La Retraite RC Girls' School, Clapham Park

God's Greatness

In just three days, God created the world we reside in,
God sent Jesus Christ to save us humans,
God saved them from persecution,
God sent angels
And saved those who were faithful,
It is by God's amazing grace we live,
And by God we recognise his sacrifice,
And through God I pray we prioritise,
And advise others to concede to God,
Accept his advice,
Comply with the faith,
Then, as my last two lines,
In Jesus' name, I pray,
Amen!

Ashaila Davis (13)
La Retraite RC Girls' School, Clapham Park

My Beautiful Truth - Black

A time to honour, a time to see,
The roots of strength in history.
From chains to crowns, we rise and stand,
A legacy built on heart and hand.

In every story, in every name,
We find our fire, we claim our flame!
Black history, rich and strong,
A vibrant song, forever long.

Harriet Tubman fled from slavery,
Guiding souls through the night, so bravely,
Black lives matter, not just in the pain,
But in every heart, in each link of the chain!

Aicha Cisse (12)
La Retraite RC Girls' School, Clapham Park

147

My Beautiful Truth Of Nigeria

My Nigeria, today is our day
A fresh start to lead the way
No control by another country
Because we have a new opportunity

Giants of Africa are what we are,
'Cause we stand proud amongst the crowds!
Come see our Ankara-
It's bright, bold and brilliant with colours!
Come hear our music,

And it will make you dance forever!
Let's go and see our jollof rice,
It's sweet, tender and nice,
It makes you jump for joy!

Audrey Oladejo (13)
La Retraite RC Girls' School, Clapham Park

My Beautiful Parents

I love the way they make me smile,
I love the way they care.
How far would I run to see them? I would run a mile!

Sometimes their love is tough,
Sometimes they make me cry,
But what I love most of all?
Their sweet love,
I will forever cherish the burnt cookies we baked!
And my mum's heels I wore!

I will never forget our love for each other,
God bless them!
Amen.

Savannah Dooknah (12)
La Retraite RC Girls' School, Clapham Park

The Truth Of My Cute Cat

My cat's eyes are as blue as the sea,
She obviously likes climbing trees,

She pounces and meows at birds in the tree,
She leaps so high, she almost flies,

She finally catches the bird in her paws,
Her nails are always sharp, they're claws!

Dinner is served, it's a real treat, well-earned,

I love her so much, she's all mine, my cat!

Khadijah Yaseen (14)
La Retraite RC Girls' School, Clapham Park

My Lineage

In October's glow, we rise and stand,
To honour the roots that shaped this land.
Stories of courage, struggle and might,
A legacy born from endless fight.

From chains to freedom, voices soar,
Breaking the silence, they open doors.
Black history lives, strong and true,
A past that paves the future anew.

Clarabelle Owusu (12)
La Retraite RC Girls' School, Clapham Park

My Beautiful Cat

My beautiful cat,
Has fluffy fur,
She always lands on her feet,
She enjoys having a treat,
Like tuna, a tasty fish,
Served in the best porcelain dish,
Cats love milk and so do I,
I love her more than seeing a rainbow in the sky,
My beautiful cat I adore,
I hope this poem has not been a bore!

Hafsah Abbasi (13)
La Retraite RC Girls' School, Clapham Park

The Truth

The truth is something unexpected because it can be good
Or bad, because it can even be harmful
This is the truth
The truth can set you free,
This is the truth
It can make you kind or mean,
This is the truth
But the truth can be anything you need,
This is the truth
The truth can change.

Amina Doumbia-Cole (12)
La Retraite RC Girls' School, Clapham Park

My Beautiful Book

My beautiful book,
Inspires dreams of adventure,
Mystery and freedom,
Sailing forever with companions that mean something
to you!
Emerging victorious in the face of adversity!
Granting freedom,
A space to breathe for many!
Smiling and positivity, even in the darkest of times!

Melodie Getaneh (12)
La Retraite RC Girls' School, Clapham Park

What If...?

Skshhhh,
I step onto the smooth surfaced ice,
My blades cutting into it with a sharp slice.
The bitter cold effortlessly stings my face into a smile,
As I miss my jacket, that's only been off a short while.
I run each motion slowly through my head,
Everything my coach had previously said.
But what if I fall? What if I rush?
I gaze at the audience, my mind melts to slush.

I think about winning, the joy after the storm,
I tell myself *be confident* and I am excited to perform.
I hear the music start to play,
As I skate better than any other day.
I smile as I don't rush, not once, not at all,
And I exit the ice without a single fall.
I am happily greeted by my friend,
Who cheered me on from start to end.

Sophie Sinha (14)

Merchant Taylors' Girls' School, Crosby

Nothing Works

I am often alone,
Or on my phone.
You cannot read my mind,
You think everything's fine.

I usually look annoyed,
But what you don't know is, I'm destroyed.
I hear others telling others to leave the world without a
trace,
Yet you still want me to think this world is a beautiful place.

I cannot be myself around any other,
Anyone besides my own mother.
I can never find anyone who I relate to,
I can never find anyone who to me is true.

In conclusion to what you have heard about me,
What you know is that my confidence is as small as a pea.
Sometimes the truth is all the best,
I will leave you all to find out the rest.

Aurora Alba (13)
Merchant Taylors' Girls' School, Crosby

Be Proud Of Ourselves

With a bright smile, joy and pride had begun.

Proud, is what we've got in joy
Proud, is an unforgettable feeling, it's a pleasure and satisfaction.
Proud, is when people went through one and another low point.

When we are proud, we smile as bright as the sun.
When we are proud, it means we've been much closer to success.
When we are proud, we cheer in happiness.

That proud smile is brighter than the sun,
That proud smile is wider than the sea
That proud smile is even warmer than the lovely heart.

Oh! What is that huge thing filled with joy and success?
That's the huge proud smile that we've given to ourselves.

Yan Nok Kristy Wong (12)
Merchant Taylors' Girls' School, Crosby

Alone With You

I like to sit and just exist,
With the stillness of my mind,
Being all by myself,
To sit and just unwind.
I'll wait and listen for a sound,
But nothing can be heard,
Not quite silence, but not a noise,
And I'll say not a word.
I find you quite the opposite,
You carry your life in your chest,
Your noise is not a droning buzz,
But more welcome than the rest.
With you, I needn't take my life force,
From the world around me,
You gift it to me freely,
And I know with you.
That I am truly me.

Isabelle Sprawson (15)
Merchant Taylors' Girls' School, Crosby

War After War

War after war! Death after death!
He jumped out, watching the carnage below,
As he descended from the air in his parachute.
He landed.

Death after death!
He ducked, dived and dodged bullets.
Blood. Blood. Blood.
Oozing and thick on the muddy, body-scattered floor.

Death after death!

The pilot scrambled across the muddy blood-soaked floor
to get a weapon.
A rifle. Shoot. Shoot. Shoot!

An enemy appears in the face of the pilot.
The pilot pulls the trigger - the enemy wins the battle.

Death. Death. Death!
The pilot hits the muddy blood-soaked floor.
Silence. Silence. Silence...

War takes another hero.

Maddox Dixon (11)
Oldbury Wells School, Oldbury Wells

159

The Beautiful Truth

Progress makes us happier
New stuff to make stuff easier
Old stuff forgotten and thrown away
We're living in a modern heyday
We iron out the world's lumpy bits
To make room for cool funky bits
But...
Sometimes we can't make the cut
Seas are rising, ice is melting
Humans are in for a real belting
Storms brewing, Earth is heating
But it's cool, we'll have a meeting
So us big guys don't get a beating
We big guys are very rich
But we want more
We act like a bitch
But the world is too sore
All our trees chopped. Gone
Rare animals starved. Gone
Because habitats. Gone
Whole eco-systems. Gone
Is it too late?
Aren't we just great?
Why is there nothing in the seas?
What happened to all the trees?
When did we last see any bees?

In a way we're all the big guy
Even though he may petrify
But progress makes us happier
New stuff to make stuff better
More cows in a field
Genetically modified to give more yield
Chickens in caged boxes
Don't have to worry about the foxes
Pigs chained to the floor
So we can have more
But the beautiful truth is raw
When the world can give no more
We cannot eat money.

Felix Davis (13)
Oldbury Wells School, Oldbury Wells

Hope

Hope is what keeps me going
It helps me to believe I will be fine
It's what drives me to become the best version of myself.

Hope is what keeps me going
It helps me to believe I'll get through my problems and worries
It's the thing that supports me to get through life.

Hope is what keeps me going
It helps me to look into my future
It's what I rely on to ensure I move forward.

Hope is what keeps me going
Without it, I am less
Without it, life feels grey
Hope brings brightness, making everything okay.

Apryl Jennings (13)
Oldbury Wells School, Oldbury Wells

Guide Us

In whispers of the warming breeze
The earth reveals a silent plea
Oceans rise and forests fade
Nature's balance, now betrayed.

The icebergs weep, their giant falls
A warning echoing through us all
Yet in the hearts of those who care
A spark ignites, a call to share.

With every step, we can reclaim
A brighter future, not just a name
Together we can turn the tide
For a healthy world, let hope be our guide.

Darcy Webb (13)
Oldbury Wells School, Oldbury Wells

Boats

Boats, beautiful boats,
How you glide through the water
Like a knife through butter.
Standing proud at the dock
Before that 'All aboard!' call,
Before you dominate the sea once more.
Boats, beautiful boats,
I hope you lead me down the sea path
I hope to go one day.

James Duncan (12)
Oldbury Wells School, Oldbury Wells

Hey Little Sister, Don't You Cry

Hey little sister, don't you cry
How about we sit and I'll sing you a lullaby
I'll read you a story, then it's time for bed
It's time to settle down and rest your head
We will turn on the night light, and watch the stars
No need to be scared, as I won't be far.

Hey little sister, don't you cry
I know you never like to say goodbye
You can help me get ready, then it's time for school
I know you, Mom, and Holly will still have a ball
Don't you worry, I'll be home soon
Then I promise we will sit and watch our cartoon.

Hey little sister, don't you cry
In a world full of noise, there's no place to be shy
It's just you, me, and Holly against the world
And we need to make sure our voices are heard
I want you to remember, that I love you from the bottom of
my heart
I will make sure that we will never be drawn apart.

Hey little sister don't you cry
I promise we will never have to say goodbye.

Aimee Cherry (12)
Park Hall Academy, Castle Bromwich

The Beautiful Truth

Like a radiant sunrise, it breaks upon the shore,
A beacon of hope, illuminating all that's more,
A truth so pure, it shines with an otherworldly glow,
A light that pierces the darkness, making the heart glow.

It whispers secrets, a gentle breeze on a summer's day,
A soft caress that stirs the soul, and chases all despair
away,
Like a masterful conductor, it orchestrates the mind,
A symphony of understanding, where harmony is aligned.

With tender fingers, it lifts the veil of deceit,
Revealing the hidden truths that our hearts had long to
greet,
Like a skilled artist, it paints a masterpiece of insight,
A canvas of clarity, where the brushstrokes of wisdom take
flight.

It personifies the power of love, a force that's strong and
free,
A liberator of the spirit, setting the heart wild and carefree,
Like a river flowing wild, it carves its path through the soul,
A journey of self-discovery, where the truth makes us whole.

With every step, it leads us closer to the heart's desire,
A destination of authenticity, where the truth sets our spirits
on fire,

Like a phoenix rising from the ashes, it transforms and renews,
A rebirth of purpose, where the truth shines bright, and all our doubts subdue.

The beautiful truth, a treasure we hold dear,
A gem that sparkles with promise, and wipes away each tear,
It's the anchor that holds trust, in the turbulent sea of life,
A guiding light that illuminates the path, and cuts through the strife.

So let us cherish this truth, this radiant and pure light,
That shines like a beacon, guiding us through the darkest of nights,
For in its beauty, we find solace, and a sense of peace that's true,
A reflection of the divine, that shines within me and you.

Tyger Willow-Steward
Park Hall Academy, Castle Bromwich

My Beautiful Truth

At school, I am surrounded by friends,
They make me laugh, they make me smile,
We all share memories together from our past,
And share stories and adventures meanwhile...

I am enclosed by strangers,
I feel destroyed and alone,
There is a cacophony of noises,
Oh, I should have known,

There is nowhere to escape,
Nowhere for me to breathe,
And absolutely nowhere
For me to be who I am meant to be,

But I'm one of those people who never wins,
And never fails to try,
Right now, I am telling you the whole truth,
Without needing to lie,

I hope that I will be fine,
I will be as calm as a midnight sea,
And I will be safe,
Around the strangers I see,

I know that I will be fine,
I will find a new me,
I'll learn to blend in,
And learn to break free,

At home, I am snug and warm,
And full of lots of love,
I feel like I can aim for the stars,
That is beyond and above,

I can play with my siblings,
And be free at last,
I'm so glad,
That my horrible fear has passed,

I can be me,
And express my inner feelings,
I am really thankful
That this is a new beginning

I'm growing now, too,
Maybe a touch too much,
But I am pleased,
That I can feel warm-hearted to the touch,

I'm learning lots now,
I am in top-set classes,
And to help me learn,
I now wear a pair of glasses,

Remember, at the start,
When I said me and my friends share stories,
This is my story,
And I am proud that I took all my opportunities.

Cherri-Marie Hughes (12)
Park Hall Academy, Castle Bromwich

169

Autumn's Testimony

There is a truth that hums beneath the skin,
Abruptly crisp, like the first autumn wind
After a desperate, sweaty summer's end,
It moves in silence where the heart has been.

Not bound by words, it lingers in the air,
In how the sun will touch the waking earth,
Or how the ocean keeps its endless vow-
A silent witness to all death, all birth.

There is a truth, like light in dawn's first breath,
That whispers through the silence of the stars,
A stillness woven in the heart of life,
Beneath the noise of days, the weight of wars.

It speaks not with the language we have known,
But in the way a tree bends to the wind,
Or how the river carves its ancient path,
Unhurried; seeking neither start nor end.

It is the pulse of time, the breath of space,
A love that hides behind all things we see,
The gentle law that binds the moon and tide,
The reflection of devotion in your eyes where I see me.

For truth is not the sharpness of a blade,
Nor certainty that fills the mind with pride.
It is the beauty of the fragile flame,
That lives and dies, yet never can divide.

To see this truth is to release the fear,
To know that all we grasp will slip away,
But in its falling, something deeper stays-
The light that guides us even in decay.

There is truth when I say,
Let us find this beauty in the dark,
In fleeting things that shimmer and depart,
For what remains, though veiled and out of sight,
Is love; the quiet fire beneath all night.

Ronita Alo (16)
Park Hall Academy, Castle Bromwich

Mother Earth's Message

"Don't worry, climate change is not a big deal."
Nobody thinks about how the polar bears feel.
Their ice caps are melting,
No one is helping.
What can we do?
"What? It's the truth."

"Don't worry, climate change is not a big deal."
Nobody thinks about how the giant pandas feel.
Their food is running low.
No one is helping though.
What can we do?
"What? It's the truth."

"Don't worry, climate change is not a big deal."
Nobody thinks about how the tigers feel.
Temperatures are changing,
Their life cycles rearranging.
What can we do?
"What? It's the truth."

"Don't worry, climate change is not a big deal."
Nobody thinks about how the elephants feel.
Temperatures are rising,
The heats are surprising.
What can we do?
"What? It's the truth."

"Don't worry, climate change is not a big deal."
Actually, it is.
What about how other people feel?
What does Mother Earth say about this?
I bet she's not excited.
I bet she's not proud.
I bet she's not delighted.
We need to speak up loud.

We will never quit.
We have one home, we need to look after it.
It's the truth.

Cordi Savage
Park Hall Academy, Castle Bromwich

My Beautiful Angel

We all have our own beautiful truths
No story is the same
So let me tell you mine
My life is in pain.

I have a beautiful angel watching down on me
Forever by my side you will always be,
I carry you through life knowing that you are there,
I think of you every day and wish you were here.

Nuvva Nanny, our guardian angel
You watch over us with care
We long to see you again
We feel lost without you there.

I know you're looking down from above
And your heart will always be filled with love,
We miss you every day
But you still guide us on our way
We have to go through life with memories that we had
And the strength you gave us even when we're sad.

For Nuvva Nanny, the loss was great
Her beauty, her grace, her love all gone, there's no debate
The world is darker, dull and grey
Without the light of Nuvva Nanny's day.

We remember, we mourn the loss of Nuvva Nanny
Forever torn,
Her beauty, her grace, her love
We will keep in our hearts where it will never sleep.

Sending signs to all the family
To show that you are still with me.
You are my Beautiful Truth
That I can guarantee.

We love you forever

Our very own Beautiful Angel.

Lilly-Anna Light (11)
Park Hall Academy, Castle Bromwich

Double Agent

The more I look into those eyes, the less I see,
I'd tell her that I love her but she knows me.
I'm pleading with the cloudy sky for what I'll be,
And it's the same old time,
My friends grow all around me, when I shrink too small,
There's a world of courage-building for a phone call.
I'll take her out where I can get more time,
Where I can stall, how long must I pine?

Put in a good word for me please,
It's been so long since I felt the breeze,
Most of her friends would leave me to freeze,
But it's different and it's strange,
Double agent.

The deeper I swim, the shallower it gets,
She kicks herself because the two of us met.
I give her everything that makes me up and yet,
She still wants me to leave.
My friends build bridges with each other up so high,
I wonder where their loyalties to me lie?
I'm left here in the rat race now to wonder why,
With this web that she weaves.

Put in a good word for me please,
It's been so long since I felt the breeze,

Most of her friends would leave me to freeze,
But it's different and it's strange,
Double agent.

Alfie Taylor (16)
Park Hall Academy, Castle Bromwich

The Beautiful Truth

Insanity breeds in the revelation of deceit.

It triggers a hyper-awareness
of deceit all around you,
and suddenly you question
everything.

A broken promise;
a ghost of a guarantee;
a truth ripped out from under your feet.

The abyss awaits.

Falling down.
Down.
Down.

To a cave of cameras -
a maze of replaying scenes
showing different sides to a story
you took for granted.

Lies carve a hollow void into your soul
that you fill with more lies,
hoping to grasp the truth,
elusive in the darkness.

It's a thirst you can't quench.
So you pour a storm into your teacup

and sip the sky's bitter tears
to restrain the roaring in your throat.

The truth is a glowing light,
a saviour,
an angel,
guiding the way,
pulling you from the depths,
lifting you up,
carrying you to safety
in its warm arms.

But the beautiful truth is a myth.
For we only realise its beauty
when we have been deceived.

We only know what we have
when it's gone.

The revelation of deceit breeds insanity.
And the abyss is always there,
waiting.

Falling down.
Down.
Down.

Libby Rodway (14)
Park Hall Academy, Castle Bromwich

World War One

War is hell,
The screaming and the bells,
Sound of gunshots ring,
The cries of men would sing.

The trenches were cold,
And the men were getting old,
People had to be bold,
People only wanted one thing.

For the war to be over,
Two minutes of silence for the dead,
From when the fields were painted red,
Rain and tears fell.

It is all a living hell,
Most men shall not return,
But the ones that do were never the same,
War shapes the people and people shape the war.

The children of the men sit at the door,
For their fathers are no more,
Some will cry, and some will sing,
And the men only want to be told one thing.

That the war is over,
And they can go home,

But for some,
They go home alone.

Codi Clark (11)

Park Hall Academy, Castle Bromwich

Equal Rights

It's 2024,
And women's rights have improved,
Although, a few things still need to change,
Women can do whatever men can do,
Yet we are still looked down on,
A woman has the same job as a man,
But gets paid less,
How is that fair?
A woman can have valid points in Parliament,
Yet there are still more men.
How is that fair?
Women are still human,
We create life,
We want careers,
We want a normal life,
Yet we are still discriminated against,
How is that fair?
It's 2024,
And women's rights have improved,
Although, a few things still need to change,
You can help change these few things,
You can help get equality for both men and women,
What will you do to help?
This saddening truth can become something so beautiful...

Roxi Steward
Park Hall Academy, Castle Bromwich

In The Trenches

Came in from France,
Dunkirk, yes from that sea,
All just to fight, to fight some damn Nazis,
Their boots and their anger marching right at me.

Here I am, stuck in the trenches,
Stood or sat on muddy ground,
There aren't even benches.
Every time a man falls
I feel my heart pound,
I will never get used to silence as a sound.

Shots fired from both sides,
Every second a man dies.
Bullets sounding pop, pop, pop,
To the floor my best friend drops.
Will the tragedy of war ever stop?

I want to soar and hear the engines roar,
Getting to new heights like never before.
For our tomorrow, they gave their today.
My great-grandad was part of this historic past,
I want to make his legacy last.

Noah Coleman (11)
Park Hall Academy, Castle Bromwich

Time Lost

Hours lost staring at a screen
Minutes passed by, was it a dream?
People speak to us, we don't hear a sound
Our thumbs do the talking, as they dance around
As we travel the world, using our apps
Our body lies still, is this a trap?

iPhone, Xbox, Nintendo Switch
So many options - which one to pick?
Playing outside could be better than this
One more game, no, I'll give that a miss
Who would have known there was so much to do?
In the real world there is always something new.

Our parents begging us to come down
I know without looking how their faces frown
Don't they know we're playing with our friends,
If we come off now our game will end
What to choose - our family or friends!

Danny Naven (12)
Park Hall Academy, Castle Bromwich

Untitled

Frozen leaves crunched underfoot
Now, the cold months of December were upon us
Fairy lights dazzled as they welcomed the Christmas spirit,
and lines of scarves and coats littered the shop windows
But how long would this last?
The weather is changing at an unstoppable pace, and will
the winter become as hot as the summer?
Maybe the comfort of hats and jumpers will soon be gone
The atmosphere is altering, so everyone needs to play their
part
Even if it is picking up the coffee cup you dropped or
running a campaign for the well-being of the environment
Do everything you can to save the planet we call home.

Rosie Faultless-Hodgson
Park Hall Academy, Castle Bromwich

The Beautiful Truth

Gymnastics is my passion,
We take pride in our actions,
I overcome my challenges,
Learning new tricks and balances.

On my journey along the way,
I was making new dreams, every day,
Sometimes I felt anxious and scared for my performance,
My new friends supported me and gave me confidence.

All the skills that I know,
I can carry it throughout my lifetime,
Gymnastics fills me with happiness and joy.

Make sure your perseverance is key,
You can be whatever you want to be,
Doesn't matter if you tumble and fall,
Use your strength and stand tall.

Lacey Palmer (11)
Park Hall Academy, Castle Bromwich

Beach Life

The soft sand in my toes,
The waves crash peacefully,
The surfers skim the waves,
Life's fantastic on the beach.

Seagulls circle high in the sky,
Ice creams melt into the sand,
Holidaymakers lounge in the sun,
Life's fantastic on the beach.

Steep sand dunes roll down to the sea,
Kids splash about in the gentle waves,
A beach ball taps between hands,
Life's fantastic on the beach.

Bodyboard in hand,
I race towards the sea,
Now it's my time to ride the waves,
Life's fantastic on the beach.

Ralph Robinson (11)
Park Hall Academy, Castle Bromwich

The Sun And Moon

In the dawn's gentle embrace, the sun awakes,
Golden rays painting the sky in warm strokes,
A radiant orb, with life it creates,
Spreading joy as the world quietly invokes,

High above, where dreams and wishes align,
The moon glimmers softly, a silver sigh,
A watchful guardian through the night's design,
Whispering secrets to the darkened sky.

Together they dance in celestial grace,
Night and day, they weave their timeless tale,
Chasing shadows, in a cosmic race,
Their light and darkness entwined without fail.

Maria Avram (13)
Park Hall Academy, Castle Bromwich

The White Rose

Amongst all flowers,
in a ruby-red field,
there stands out
a singular special rose.

Colourless but beautiful,
real but also fanciful,
it's a rose that has
a forgotten kind of beauty.

Adored by many,
but truly appreciated by few if any,
the natural crossbow,
filling the rose with sorrow.

A rose that glows,
in the ebony night,
and dances beneath
the bright moonlight.

Amongst all flowers,
in a ruby-red field,
there stands out
a unique unpigmented rose.

Phoebe Matthews (12)
Park Hall Academy, Castle Bromwich

189

Life Is Like A Circle

Life is like a circle, the beginning of something new
When the sun glows the moon is a shade of blue
From baby steps to running fast
Each moment never lasts

In the beginning it's all play
While playing we will laugh all day
From net to zone to hoop
Life is a loop

As we grow we pave our way
Chasing dreams as we may
Sometimes we fall, sometimes we rise
All of our fails make us more wise

As the circle of life spins around
It doesn't matter where we wound
Everyone gets confused and thinks how
The only thing that matters is now.

Chase Wiseman
Park Hall Academy, Castle Bromwich

Cool To Be Kind

Everybody is unique and different in their own way.
You may be tall, short or even gay.
You may wear glasses, enjoy reading books.
Meeting up with friends, taking care of your looks.
You might be shy, too scared to say 'hi'.
Your clothes may look different from all the rest.
But it's your choice how you dress.
You may be sporty or a bit of a 'geek'.
But that doesn't mean you're weak.
We don't know what's on people's minds.
Remember we are different and it's cool to be kind.

Poppy-May Addison (12)
Park Hall Academy, Castle Bromwich

The Beautiful Truth

In shadows deep, where silence dwells
A fragile spark that softly glows
With weary steps, we tread the ground
In search of light, where hope is found.

For in the dark, resilience breeds
And from despair, the spirit feeds
With every dawn, a promise new
That hope will rise and carry through.

So let us walk, though shadows loom
With hearts ablaze, dispelling gloom
In every struggle, let us find
The light of hope that guides the mind.

Niamh Watkins (11)
Park Hall Academy, Castle Bromwich

The World Of Nature

Look at the nature around us,
Our ecosystem is enormous,
That's why we have to keep it clean,
Living in a world that's clean is a dream.

But some people disobey,
And the world doesn't feel like a holiday,
The streets get filled with litter,
And I want people to reconsider.

There used to be nature everywhere,
But now the world is a nightmare,
We can't flee because
There is no Planet B.

Isabel Goodhall (12)
Park Hall Academy, Castle Bromwich

A Soldier Lost At War

Beneath a sky of smoke and shattered stars,
The earth, once soft, now trembles under fire.
A soldier's heartbeat through the scars,
His breath a whisper caught on a barbed wire.
The distant cries of home feel far away,
Like memories dissolving in the rain.
He wonders if the dawn will bring the day,
Or if the night will cradle all his pain.
Yet still he marches, broken but alive,
In war, the hope is to simply survive.

Maleehah Millwala (12)
Park Hall Academy, Castle Bromwich

Untitled

The things I believe,
And the things I want to achieve,
Row in harmony,
Down the river of 'I believe',
As far as my future goes,
I aspire high,
And as for low,
Well, I don't want to go that far,
When I grow up
I want to be a teacher,
And hopefully I'll meet ya,
The things I believe
And the things I want to achieve,
Conceive in harmony!

Macie Veitch (13)

Park Hall Academy, Castle Bromwich

A Beautiful Truth

What a beautiful truth
Two foxes sit side by side, set ablaze with copper and
crimson
Their fur contrasting with the setting sun bubbling into the
horizon
The delicate touch of their paws pattering on the silky sand
Footsteps dissolved into the ocean like sugar in tea
Trees cast erratic silhouettes onto the land
And their tails whipped through the wind
Oh, what a beautiful truth.

Ruby Anthony (13)
Park Hall Academy, Castle Bromwich

The Beautiful Truth Of Someone's Unique Identity

Everyone is unique in their own way,
And that is what makes them beautiful,
No one should be treated differently,
As we are all the same,
Though we may look different,
We all are born, bleed, and die the same.

Leo Allen-Perks (12)
Park Hall Academy, Castle Bromwich

One More

One more football game,
As they cheer my wonderful name,
One more pair of boots I'll wear,
Lots of presents with paper to tear,
One more kit I'll choose,
This is the game I don't want to lose,
One more team win,
I'll have a big grin,
One more man of the match,
Okay, let's have a rematch.

Ariana Wall (11)
Park Hall Academy, Castle Bromwich

Everyone Matters!

E rase racism and conflict,

Q uantity doesn't matter,

U nited is what we need to be,

A nd so everyone should be free,

L ive altogether in peace,

I n a group, when in your youth,

T his is the beautiful truth,

Y ou can be a part of it.

Nancy Jane McKinley (12)

Park Hall Academy, Castle Bromwich

My Beautiful Truths

Eleven years of age
Ten hopes for the future
Nine favourite desserts
Eight favourite subjects
Seventh year of education
Six close family members
Five minutes of reflection each day
Four best friends
Three dreams
Two dogs
One sister
Zero worries.

Rose Ellis-Mayes
Park Hall Academy, Castle Bromwich

The Blossom Tree

The pink, pretty blossom tree sits upon the misty hills,
Standing tall and brave, and ready to bloom during the
summer heat,
This blossom tree sits upon the English coast,
Rain, rain, go away try and feed me in another way!

Ava Saunders (12)
Park Hall Academy, Castle Bromwich

The Beautiful Truth

Football is the best sport in the world
Because you get lots of money
And you will get famous
And everyone will be cheering you,
There will also be a big stadium
With over 100,000 people inside.

Bobbie Bluck (12)
Park Hall Academy, Castle Bromwich

Is It Okay?

"Stray Kids, everywhere, all around the world.
You make Stray Kids stay."

Forever doesn't exist
And that's okay.

Humaira Amiri (16)
Park Hall Academy, Castle Bromwich

Beautiful Truth

In the quiet golden dawn, before the world wakes from its slumber,
Truth treads softly, with steps that shake the Earth beneath its gentle stride,
Yet moves so lightly, it is hard to encounter it boldly.

It is the silver thread in the weave of night,
The quiet murmur in the fading light.
Neither harsh nor cruel, it humbly waits,
Beyond the boundaries of Time or Fate.

For Truth is not the sword, destructive and cold,
Nor the burden of secrets left untold.
It does not shout in the market square,
But whispers softly in the open air.

It lives in the way the rain kisses the fertile ground,
In every heartbeat, a rhythmic sound.
It is found in the eyes of those who see,
That life, in all its pain, is free.
There is beauty in the scars we bear,
In the dreams we hold, in the love we share.

For Truth, at its core, is simply this:
An endless longing for pure bliss.

It resides not in grandeur and splendour,
But in moments when no one cares -

In the fleeting smile, in a quiet sigh,
In the way we love, and the way we cry.

It is not perfection, nor is it a flaw,
But it is the softness of a hand, that reaches out in times of
need,
A tender act, a selfless deed.
It is the honesty in a tear, the courage found in facing fear.
It is found in hearts that break and mend,
In love that grows but doesn't end.
It is ultimately the peace that comes from within,
When we embrace life as it has been.

The beautiful truth, so hard to find,
Is often latent in the mind.
Yet it lingers, within the self, humming a melody only the
soul can hear.
And when at last we see it clear, it is not a scream, but a
gentle tear.
For truth, when embraced, is absolute bliss and kind -
A halo of light within the heart and mind.
A steady, unwavering flame, both warm and bright
Leading us towards the heavenly light.

Aadya Sinha (11)
Upton Court Grammar School, Slough

205

The Beautiful Truth

The beautiful truth,
Is that no one has eternal youth.
Life will never be a steady cruise,
With every win, there's a loss.
Seasons will change in the blink of an eye,
As days, weeks, years fly by.
Making you wish time would cease,
Wish that the wrinkles would decrease,
But the beautiful truth,
Is that no one has eternal youth,
And yes, it will make you feel unease,
But on the bright side, it will make you seize
Fulfilling memories with them all,
Hugs, kisses, cries and brawls,
So when you look back to the good old days.
Those beautiful memories will keep you in a daze,
And when those meaningful mortals disappear,
You'll be left with downcast and joyful tears,
Remembering those memories, you made long ago,
Like how you laughed with them in the snow,
Happiness with them couldn't be measured,
That person, that love, was such a rare treasure,
That gives such a warm feeling remembering them,
And will stimulate the recollections, will make them all stem,
The fun, the worst, the cheers, the cries,
Making you think maybe, maybe, if we had one more time,

But no, this is the beautiful truth,
No one has eternal youth,
So, when I am gone, remember me,
Not with tears, sorrow and plea,
But with a smile, at the moments we made,
Which, over time, will start to fade,
As you move on, as time passes by,
Whilst our souls reach for each other between the two skies,
One day meeting together, grasping forever.
Because the beautiful truth,
Is that no one has eternal youth.

Aysha Anfaz (17)
Upton Court Grammar School, Slough

The Beautiful Truth

What is the most beautiful truth?
A sentence you hear that alters your brain?
A word you read that makes you believe?
A phrase you see as you pass by a wall filled with graffiti?
Is it religion? The truth of life?
Science? Existence?
Art? Love?
How can a truth be beautiful?
Why would it be?
For we are submerged in a world full of lies,
Hatred and brutality,
Everyone lies,
Everyone discriminates,
Everyone has screamed and kicked and fought and cried,
We lie and say that the world isn't burning,
That we love our neighbours and forgive those who have
wronged us,
We want peace and love throughout all mankind,
When really our hearts are blind,
Blind with rage and jealousy,
Anger and immorality,
We lie and say that we feel at peace,
With religion and nature,
That we have souls and a good heart,
A heart with the ability to be pure,
Maybe I'm exaggerating, maybe I'm not,

For all I've seen is a world full of hatred,
A world full of lies,
A world full of war and fights,
A world filled with corruption and criminals,
But honestly,
I think the most beautiful truth,
Is the lie.

Andra-Elena Seghete (16)
Upton Court Grammar School, Slough

The Beautiful Truth

The beautiful truth,
A whisper so pure,
Where doubts are bound,
To endure.
In the silence,
It gleams as a sun,
A light emitted,
From all the day's fun.

The beautiful truth,
Is a mesmerising mystery.
It's one's future,
And another's history
Like the stars,
High in the sky,
It teaches some to trust,
And some to lie.

The beautiful truth,
Is an invisible entity.
Where one can locate,
Their identity.
It hides in the ordinary,
Small and bright.
In the flicker of stars,
In the softest light.

The beautiful truth,
Resides in a gentle grace.
Lives in the silence,
Yet finds every face.
Whether the world crashes or bends,
It will arise again.

Open your narrow eyes to glimpse,
Subtle glow,
Whether it shall rain,
Or snow,
The beautiful truth,
Once again will flow.

Rishabh Singhaniya (12)
Upton Court Grammar School, Slough

The Beautiful Truth

Words only deceive,
Eyes only perceive,
Who knows? I know.
I see the world as a junction,
A junction for pain and success;
Like a seed waiting to bloom,
Guilty or not, I stand in the way.
I mark my ground.

I shall not be moved
Not until the end.

Beauty differs, person by person, week by week
But it is eternally sweet
In the dear sphere we stay on.
It changes to all,
It can be wrapped in the pages of a book.
An escape from the everyday.
No clue about you.
Still, sorrows sweep stillness,
And I watch the wind,
As truth is weighed over.
On a mountain in the sky.
They want me to forget.
I always remember…

Mahi Gupte (13)
Upton Court Grammar School, Slough

The Beautiful Truth

In the silent dusk, where murmurs blend,
The heart shows what words cannot lend,
The beautiful truth needs to come to light,
One that the darkness cannot fight,

Upon the canvas of a radiant night,
The beautiful truth readies its wind and takes flight,
Love shall ignite in all's heart,
Until we rest in peace and part,

In times of darkness, a light shall gleam,
In every ending, a beginning, and a distant dream,
As truth is found, in the smallest of things,
Like someone's smile, the joy it brings.

Kiaan Maniar (12)
Upton Court Grammar School, Slough

YOUNG WRITERS INFORMATION

We hope you have enjoyed reading this book – and that you will continue to in the coming years.

If you're the parent or family member of an enthusiastic poet or story writer, do visit our website **www.youngwriters.co.uk/subscribe** and sign up to receive news, competitions, writing challenges and tips, activities and much, much more! There's lots to keep budding writers motivated!

If you would like to order further copies of this book, or any of our other titles, then please give us a call or order via your online account.

Young Writers
Remus House
Coltsfoot Drive
Peterborough
PE2 9BF
(01733) 890066
info@youngwriters.co.uk

**Join in the conversation!
Tips, news, giveaways and much more!**

f YoungWritersUK **X** YoungWritersCW

@ youngwriterscw **♪** youngwriterscw